THE WHISTLEBLOWER

Rooting for the Ref in the High-Stakes

World of College Basketball

BOB KATZ

ForeEdge

ForeEdge

An imprint of University Press of New England

www.upne.com

© 2015 Bob Katz

All rights reserved

Manufactured in the United States of America

Designed by Mindy Basinger Hill

Typeset in Chaparral Pro

For permission to reproduce any of the material in this book,

contact Permissions, University Press of New England,

One Court Street, Suite 250, Lebanon NH 03766;

or visit www.upne.com

Hardcover ISBN: 978-1-61168-451-3

Ebook ISBN: 978-1-61168-710-1

Library of Congress Control Number: 2014946020

5   4   3   2   1

For my father, the fairest man I've ever known

CONTENTS

Illustrations follow page 112.

The "invisible gorilla experiment" is a fascinating investigation of what cognitive psychologists term "selective attention." The experiment, which consists of the rapid passing of a basketball between two groups of moving players, demonstrates how easily people lapse into the assumption that they clearly see, and definitively know, more than they actually do.

Devised by Christopher Chabris and Daniel Simons, both Harvard University psychologists at the time, the experiment asked participants to watch a video in which two groups of players, one wearing black shirts and another wearing white, men and women, three in each group, freely pass two separate basketballs among themselves. Besides their T-shirts, these players are dressed in casual street clothes, mostly jeans. While passing the balls, they weave in and out of a tight circle in irregular routes, black and white intermingling, sometimes seeming to get in each other's way, as if ineptly performing a rudimentary drill meant to teach teamwork to basketball beginners.

"Count how many times the players wearing white pass the basketball," is the one instruction given to the participants in the study. The video runs for half a minute.

Midway through the video, a costumed gorilla clad in head-to-toe fake fur and a dark, leathery face, strolls leisurely into the circle of players, stands for a moment, beats his chest, and then exits. Participants were later asked, "Did you see the gorilla?" More than half did not.

This much-admired experiment, an Internet sensation with ten million views on YouTube as of this writing, has become a staple of cognitive psychology courses and is being adapted for instructional use in various professions, like radiology, that place a premium on a practitioner's powers of observation. For those, like me, who fastidiously kept track of each time the basketball was being passed among white shirts yet somehow managed to overlook the conspicuous presence of a Halloween gorilla that strutted dead center into the visual field, the study served as a vivid demonstration that the perceptual skills on which we so greatly rely are, to put it mildly, far from flawless.

"Our intuition is that we will notice something that's visible, that's distinctive," explained psychologist Simons. "And that intuition is consistently wrong."

The fan sees what he wants to see is a standard cliché of the sports world, and for good reason. But it is also true that we see mainly what we've learned to see, been taught to see, been habituated into believing *is all there is* to see.

Might there be more?

Initially, I would have thought, sure, of course there may be more, but who needs it? Sports fans, like fast-food patrons, generally know what we like and know where to get it. For me, basketball, particularly college basketball with its youthful enthusiasms, exuberant play, and compelling geographical rivalries, has always done the trick. I flop onto the couch, diddle the remote, and presto! Like a cartoon character blasted to another realm, I've escaped the cloying annoyances of the dull and nagging universe, otherwise known as reality, and entered a dazzling world of breathtaking athleticism ruled by an unforgiving clock relentlessly ticking down toward victory or defeat. Any human quest that must ultimately conclude in unambiguous victory or defeat will grab my attention, and probably yours.

But there can come a time in a sports fan's career — do fans indeed have "careers"? Yes, by God, I believe we do! — when circumstances unexpectedly conspire and suddenly you're open to a fresh perspective. For me, it came on during the depths of midwinter malaise, and the weather was only part of the problem. Maybe I'd seen too many games that particular season. Maybe the surplus of camera close-ups depicting dapper coaches in high dudgeon had left me feeling a tad alienated. At any rate, I rubbed my eyes while watching a game, and when my vision cleared, bingo! There it was, in stark black and white, almost begging for a tryout. The ref, I realized, was the gorilla on the court.

Watch any game long enough and invariably there will be reason to take notice, often with exasperation or a reaction more acute. That lonely figure scampering the boundaries of the hardwood, dressed in zebra shirt with silver whistle dangling, may not be the center of the action, but he is far from absent.

Of course, I'd seen the ref. What fan who claims to call himself a fan has not?

There are, however, multiple implications to the invisible gorilla experiment findings. Chabris and Simons point out that their research "reveals two things: that we are missing a lot of what goes on around us, and that we have no idea that we are missing so much." In other words, we cannot see it all and we are affected by the false assumption that we mostly can.

Even unsympathetic fans generally understand that the referee, inundated by a sea of distractions, is vulnerable to overlooking actions, even seemingly obvious ones, that can occur during the course of a game. But what, I wondered, might we, the fans, be missing by overlooking the referee?

THE WHISTLEBLOWER

The first nationally televised college basketball game Ed Hightower ever refereed was Michigan State versus the University of Iowa, in Iowa City on January 5, 1983. He was thirty-one years old and just beginning to work his way into a regular rotation of choice assignments in brand-name conferences like the Big Ten and the Missouri Valley Conference. An ebullient man with a welterweight's compressed muscularity, he'd come up the hard way — harder than almost anyone could imagine — and it pleased him to know that friends and family back in southern Illinois could tune in to watch him work. At least someone would be rooting for him.

All sporting contests are to some extent a stage, and there's nothing quite like national TV coverage to emphasize this point. Players like to say they just ignore the extra attention, and more power to them if they actually manage to do so. Top-tier coaches, like skilled actors, know precisely where the camera is and how to play to it. As for the referees, well, nobody much likes to consider what they're thinking since the whole experience of organized sports is neater, cleaner, and infinitely more palatable if the referees can be altogether ignored. In a perfect world, they might not even be needed.

The game was hard fought throughout. Michigan State was one of the nation's top teams and featured three athletes — Sam Vincent, Scott Skiles, and Kevin Willis — who would go on to careers in the NBA. Iowa, led by future pros Bobby Hansen and

Greg Stokes, kept the game close. The pace was fast and furious, yet Hightower had no difficulty keeping up: the elite-conference supervisors who'd finally begun assigning him some important games understood that his promising set of skills included the ability to run, to really flat-out run. Although never a star in his own playing days, Hightower retained an athlete's capacity to accelerate without warning, maybe not always quickly enough to match the swiftness of a nimble guard speeding away with a steal but fast enough, when combined with shrewd anticipation of the plausible patterns of developing plays, and the implausible ones as well, to arrive in the nick of time at the optimal vantage point. Players hustle to beat their man down court; refs hustle to get properly positioned for whatever happens next.

Hightower was certainly not one to be left lagging. A driven man with a ferocious work ethic, he was keenly aware there were no guarantees in this profession and plenty of potential pitfalls. It had been several years getting this far. The path to advancement in basketball officiating parallels that of other professions. The lower rungs are denoted by grade-school and rec-league games in under-heated gyms with nobody but a handful of rankled parents watching. The next steps involve working high school and lower-level college contests where the pace and pressure quicken. Any flaw in an official's skill set, be it temperament or judgment or the intangible aptitude for managing the mayhem, soon gets exposed. The top rung consists of working marquee matchups between Division 1 teams in elite conferences. These assignments pose greater levels of difficulty and promise greater rewards, including compensation and prestige. Successfully ascending the officiating ladder involves all the elements that contribute to success in other fields — talent, dedication, perseverance, ambition, timing, and a certain amount of luck.

Prior to the 1983 season, Hightower had been refereeing junior colleges in Illinois and Missouri. Those assignments had been a distinct upgrade from the high school contests he'd been working previously in the basketball-crazed towns on the Illinois side of the Mississippi River, towns like Belleville, Alton, Collinsville, East St. Louis, and Granite City. Until this season, his officiating career had been spent entirely in dimly lit, under-heated, claustrophobic gyms that rarely seated more than a few hundred. None of the games in those venues were televised.

Not all refs approach their career with a burning determination to make it to the top. The chances of getting there are slim, and plenty of satisfaction, along with some supplemental income, can be had in the lower circuits. But for the ambitious ones, the goal is to be selected to officiate the most important games, where the stakes are highest, where the pressure is greatest. Getting there is always a long shot. Staying there is often a greater challenge than getting there. Working a national TV game, as Hightower was well aware, can amount to a big career break. Such occasions provide an aspiring ref with the opportunity to be seen looking the part, acting the part, proudly comporting himself in that crisp and authoritative manner that declares to all relevant stakeholders — players, coaches, fans — worry not: the rules tonight will be fairly enforced, and the playing field will not be allowed to tilt in either direction.

On the other hand, screwing up on national TV can trigger a quick trip to oblivion.

. . .

With five seconds left, Iowa prepared to pass the ball inbounds, trailing 61–59. Throughout this seesaw contest, Hightower had been getting it in measured doses from the two coaches — a stifled squawk, a pantomimed plea, an expertly timed howl of exasperation. Their full-bore, enraged bull, hell-hath-no-fury protest was, he knew, being saved for later when it would matter most. Later was now.

Millions were watching on TV. It was the dawn of the cable explosion. ESPN was still in its infancy. There was no Fox Sports with its sprawling Pacific, Central, and Atlantic coverage, and conference-specific networks like we have now in the Big Ten, ACC, SEC, and Pac-12 had yet to be devised. Whereas local stations often had arrangements to occasionally televise local college games, the network TV weekend broadcasts were, prior to the year-end NCAA tournament, the only national telecasts that afforded college basketball fans from around the country a chance to view important non-regional games.

Billy Packer was the CBS announcer for Hightower's TV debut that early January afternoon in Iowa City. During a span of over thirty years, stretching until 2008, Packer was the voice most closely identified with college basketball. And his was quite a voice — mellifluous, enthusiastic, opinionated, articulate, careening wildly as the game itself careened, professorial one moment, fanatical the next. These days, a referee's worst nightmare is to suffer some momentary lapse in judgment, or simply an unavoidable bad bounce of the sort that are rife throughout all sports, and have it memorialized in seeming perpetuity on ESPN's *SportsCenter* replays. Back in the day, it was having Billy Packer's cocksure voice second-guessing a questionable call, gnawing away at the alleged malfeasance.

Every ref knows he could be one ugly sequence away from the purgatory of everlasting castigation. Officiating blunders that affect the outcome can become a spiraling descent into perpetual vilification straight out of Dante: mess up an important call, get pummeled by the broadcasters during the ensuing break, get flayed by TV recaps following the game and, these days, wind up endlessly crucified by Internet bloggers who don't know the meaning of the statute of limitations.

Lute Olson was the Iowa coach. He would eventually move to the University of Arizona where he'd go on to win a national championship. Olson had risen in the coaching ranks the old-fashioned way, one humble step at a time. His first thirteen years as a coach were spent far from the main stage, at Mahnomen and Two Rivers High Schools in rural Minnesota.

The Michigan State coach, George Melvin "Jud" Heathcoate, was cut from the same cloth, having spent fourteen seasons coaching high school hoops in Spokane before getting the opportunity to direct the freshman squad at nearby Washington State University (at the time, NCAA rules did not permit freshmen to play on the college varsity). Being named Michigan State head coach had marked a huge leap forward for Heathcoate, and he did not waste time. His third season in East Lansing, the Spartans, led by Magic Johnson, would win the national championship in the fabled match-up against Indiana State's Larry Bird.

Heathcoate and Olsen, it's safe to say, were each familiar with the tactic known generically as "working the ref," that is, utilizing an array of communication tools, from silent scowl to full-throated, foot-stomping outrage, with the hope of coaxing the ref into eventually seeing the game, and in particular the alleged subterfuges of the opposing team, precisely the way the coach wants him to see it. Instilling a momentary flicker of empathy into a stubborn ref's subconscious just might make the difference at some critical juncture. Or so coaches like to believe.

The relationship between college coaches and the referees working their games is one of the strangest imaginable, fraught with simmering tensions. Coaches are the bane of referees. In any given season, in any given game, at any important interlude, real or imagined, it is the coach who can seem to care the most, who is *paid* to care the most, and who wants the ref to never forget how desperately he cares. Coaches want to win. They are hired to win. Winning is how they keep their jobs. The obstacles to winning are varied and too often outside their control. The mercurial judgments of referees, in the minds of many coaches, represent yet another form of misfortune that's always threatening to bring them down. Throughout the game, this attitude gets expressed in a series of exchanges that are subtly coded until, without warning, they explode into something so explicit that even spectators in the nosebleed seats understand perfectly well what is being communicated. What refs and coaches have in common is a love for the game. And that's about it. Temperamentally, they are nearly opposite.

Refs are professionally dispassionate, objective, outwardly calm, broad-minded, conciliatory, adaptable, accepting of contradiction. Coaches tend to be fiery, visibly tense, high-strung, hyper-competitive type A's prone to egocentric perspectives on any dispute not resolved in their favor. They are also extraordinarily talented influencers of others. The charitable term for these qualities when trained on their squad of young athletes is "motivational" or even "inspiring." That same talent for passionate fist-pounding insistence on what ought to be done might, when directed at the officials, be called "manipulation." Or attempted manipulation. From the opening tip to the crucial action at game's end, the best coaches are trying to get into the referee's head, to slyly infiltrate his perceptions. And nowhere is this as true as with a neophyte ref just breaking into the big time who might not yet be inured to their entire bag of devious tricks.

It could make a neat setup for a clever HBO drama (or comedy), a wily coach and a veteran ref stranded together in a remote jungle outpost, forced to work through a tangled history of bitter disputes in order to find the common ground and shared values necessary for survival. Can they come together and find a basis for trust? Stay tuned.

Iowa guard Steve Carfino took the inbounds pass. The capacity crowd of over 15,000 rose to its feet, shrieking encouragement. The Iowa fans had been in a celebratory mood all day, as this was the very first game ever played in the brand new $18.5 million Carver Arena. The noise was skull rattling. Frantic players jostled, seeking an edge.

Until this point, Hightower felt he'd had a good game. There'd been a twinge of indecision on one or two calls in the paint, and another on a who-touched-the-ball-last deflection out-of-bounds. These might occasion some reflection later, after the game. But if he'd made mistakes, and it was virtually impossible to work an entire forty-minute game without a few errors, he felt certain none were of real significance, and none had impinged on the balance of the game or bestowed an unfair advantage on either team. Referees approach each game with a very explicit goal in mind. They want to create conditions, though their officiating, that will enable the team that plays the best that day to have a fair chance to win. That elementary formulation is all they can realistically hope to accomplish, and it is a mission in which they take immense pride.

In principle, it sounds simple: to create conditions that allow the team playing best to have a fair shot at winning. And in principle it probably is. It's the actual *practice* of administering fairness in such a contentious environment that proves anything but simple. And in the final minutes of a tight game that could swing either way or, as in this case, the final *seconds*, in which whatever happens next will likely decide who wins, there would be no room for error. And nowhere to hide.

Nor would there be any video review available. That marvelous technological tool, both blessing and curse, would not become a staple of college basketball officiating until a few years later.

Hightower, a gregarious man with a beaming smile that should not be mistaken for an eagerness to please, perfectly understood this was crunch time. Quietly, he did a little Zen-like clearing of his mind. *Be prepared*, he told himself. *Anticipate yet don't get locked in by assumptions. Think but don't overthink.*

So many calls must be made almost instantaneously. Yet the human capacity to process fragmented information at lightning speeds may not always be fully up to the task. "Referees do not perceive and record things perfectly, like a video camera could," explained Dan Simons, cocreator of the invisible gorilla experiment and a professor of psychology at University of Illinois whose research focuses on the cognitive underpinnings of our perception of the "continuous" visual world. "Refs must make judgment calls about rapid events and in some cases they will have to guess based on partial information. Some of those judgment calls are going to be wrong. We can spread our attention over multiple things at the same time," Simons added. "But there are limits on that."

Carfino dribbled furiously up-court, with Hightower just behind, tracking the action from the trail position. Under pressure from the Michigan State defense, Carfino rifled a pass to Bobby Hansen cutting toward the sideline. A smooth-shooting 6'6" guard who would later team with Michael Jordan on the NBA championship Chicago Bulls, Hansen grabbed the ball, rotated, and in one swift, seamless extension of arm and wrist let it fly from just beyond the three-point line, newly instituted that season.

The shot looked true. The crowd — do we even have to spell it out? — went ab-so-lute-ly nuts.

But Ed Hightower saw something. Or thought he saw something. Tracking the play from the trail position, it appeared to him that Carfino's sneaker had grazed the out-of-bounds line as he was zipping the ball to Hansen. *Might have grazed the line* is the way most of us would characterize the observation, for under such chaotic conditions — ear-shattering noise, skittering motion of large frenzied bodies, the unnerving aura of mass desperation — how can anyone be absolutely certain of something so imprecise? Before actually making the call, before tweeting his whistle (not that anyone would hear), before repeatedly chopping his arm to signal that the ball should go the opposite way, there was an instant when Hightower realized that the shot he was poised to nullify, this final attempt by the adored home-team Hawkeyes, was destined to be the game winner.

In that fleeting moment, he recognized how very easy it would be to ignore the perceived out-of-bounds infraction. Perhaps he did not see what he thought he saw. A non-call would be entirely plausible. Nobody could doubt his sincerity in abstaining. That rangy Iowa shooter had made an amazing shot, simple as that. Fifteen thousand fans were already erupting with that special euphoric joy that only the improvisational magic of sports can produce. Why spoil the party? Hightower could have been mistaken. Whatever happened had happened (or not) in a blur, in a flash. Blink of an eye.

Veteran referees with a history of stellar performance in big games enjoy some latitude with league supervisors. Mistakes happen. Refereeing is a consummately imperfect human activity, as is the playing of the game itself. Even LeBron has missed clutch shots. Everybody involved with competitive sports — coaches, players, fans, media — would prefer that officiating be performed with machinelike precision. But until that day arrives, it remains an art, not a science. And newer refs, like fledgling playwrights, are especially vulnerable to negative reviews. Hightower had been warned that one very unfortunate call in one unlucky situation, one bad call in one bad spot, especially at the end of a game, can derail a young ref's career. Well, here he was.

But he had seen, or thought he'd seen, a violation. And there was

no time to evaluate the ephemeral evidence. Speak now or forever
. . . Hightower blew a shrill tweet. He put air in the whistle, as the
refs like to say. With outstretched hand, he emphatically pointed,
down, down, straight at the black strip of sideline he was now
accusing Carfino's errant foot of having nicked: out-of-bounds!

The crowd of 15,000 did in fact erupt . . . but not with joy.

A storm of booing swept across the arena. Full-throated out-
cries, burning with unquenchable hurt, rained down. Hightower
braced for the inevitable next stage of onslaught.

An enraged Coach Olson stormed his way. Shockingly, however,
Olson dashed right past him, straight to the scorer's table. Olson,
it turned out, was simply in a rush to determine exactly where the
game clock had stood at the precise instant of Carfino's sideline
violation. He wanted to know how much time remained.

Braced for Olsen's onslaught, Hightower was slow to realize that
what he'd received was a tacit concession. There would be no hys-
terical outburst from the Iowa bench. There would be no threats,
veiled or otherwise. On the contrary, he'd just been exonerated.
Olson's response could not have been more pleasing if he'd joyously
slapped Hightower on the back with congratulations. There would
be no appeal. He'd nailed the call.

Many of the skills that are instrumental to successful officiating, like knowing the rules and understanding the permutations
of the game, can be diligently achieved through enough practice
and real-world experience. But the big one, the crucial one, the
heart-and-soul skill without which any aspiring referee is forever
doomed to mediocrity and all the displeasure that goes with it,
is decisiveness.

Later, as his career progressed and took shape, Hightower would
look back on this game as a pivotal experience, for the trial by fire
he'd survived but also for a new self-image it allowed him to try
on and see how it fit. He was now convinced he was very good at

this. Refereeing and the attributes it demanded—the physical exertion, the acumen on the fly, the knowledge of the rulebook and the dexterity needed to enforce it, the courage to assert his judgment, the humility to recognize his limitations—represented a sizable challenge, one that got his juices going. No two games were alike. The arena, the play, the players, the coaches, the situational pressures, the host of wholly unpredictable quirks, always required an impromptu approach. Every game required deviation from the game plan. He had to be clear-eyed and alert to the moment, with all senses trained on the ceaselessly shifting jigsaw, ten players, two coaches, one ball. Officiating a basketball game was problem solving of a very high order. Each game presented a new and fascinating chance to succeed. Or fail.

Sportswriters are fond of recounting, almost reverentially, the prophetic words of the legendary baseball slugger Ted Williams, who early in his extraordinary career boldly asserted, "All I want out of life is that when I walk down the street folks will say, 'There goes the greatest hitter who ever lived.'"

What Ed Hightower aspired to was almost comparably immodest. He wanted those rabid, tenacious, monomaniacal, take-no-prisoner, victory-at-any-cost, alpha-male coaches to eventually say of him, "He's the ref I want working the game when we're playing on the road."

IN A VERY PARTISAN PLACE

Ed Hightower was a name only vaguely known to me when I began exploring the world of college basketball referees. He was a referee who'd only avoided complete anonymity by virtue of the vast number of high-profile games he'd officiated over a long career. I couldn't have told you what he looked like or what, if any, telltale proclivities he possessed. His was just a name that had been repeated over and over in the fuzzy background of the semi-stupor of my sports viewing. Somehow the name had stuck. He'd reffed the national championship game four times, including some vintage classics, and the Final Four twelve times, with a remarkable stretch of seven straight Final Four appearances tucked in there. He was a mainstay of major conferences, especially the Big Ten, Big Twelve, Big East, and Missouri Valley, whose games were frequently televised. Had he done something glorious or dastardly once upon a time? Or was he every bit as nondescript as his nameless brethren? Search me. His was just one of those names — the world of sports is strewn with them — that popped up periodically and retained a foggy familiarity.

I mention this by way of explaining that my initial reasons for contacting Hightower, of all the refs I might have approached, were not especially calculated or well thought out. His day job (most college refs, unlike their NBA brethren, have other employment) was one that made him perhaps a bit easier than most to locate.

Hightower was the superintendent of schools of Edwardsville,

Illinois, a semirural community across the Mississippi River from St. Louis. A day job as the person in charge of an entire school district, with all the moving pieces that invariably involved, struck me as a potentially illuminating parallel, and contrast, to being a college basketball referee, although I could not have told you exactly why.

I called Hightower up. It was early August. School was not in session. The basketball season, during which he was routinely working as many as seventy games a year, would not begin for several months. His cordial secretary put me on hold. Then she came back on the line to take a message. He was busy.

It took a few days to get a call back. Even in what I imagined to be the August doldrums, he had many issues to wrestle with. The Edwardsville teachers were threatening a walkout at the start of the coming term over contract matters. The state of Illinois was further reducing its allotment to the district, and budget cuts were inevitable. Bus routes and class schedules needed to be revised, and not everyone was happy.

Eventually I went to visit. Edwardsville's school-district headquarters are housed in a converted mansion built in 1875 by the town's leading banker and benefactor, W. F. L. Hadley. Hightower's office occupies what was once the opulent front parlor, with tall windows looking out on lovely, tree-lined St. Louis Street with its stately Queen Anne, Italianate, and Greek revival homes dating from the mid-late nineteenth century. Greeting me with a hearty handshake, Hightower could himself have passed for a successful banker. Dressed impeccably in a dapper charcoal suit, white shirt, and lavender tie, he had the beaming smile and crisp cordiality of someone adept at welcoming people into his world without letting them forget who's in charge. Even in his tailored suit, he looked vigorous and fit, an ex-athlete ready to jump right in and mix it up.

Books lined the mantel of the marble fireplace. Their titles represented, sincerely yet also deliberately, values with which he wanted to be associated — *Good to Great*, *The Experience Economy*, *The Last Lecture*, *Real Change Leadership*, biographies of Ben Franklin and Stan Musial. Mementos of his basketball life were on display — photos of him being harangued on the court by Bobby Knight and Rick Pitino, an engraved plaque honoring him for officiating the World Championship of Basketball in Argentina — but these took a distinct backseat to the business at hand, stacks of budget reports, rolled-up architectural plans for a school renovation, his phone console perpetually buzzing even in the dog days of August.

Hightower's superintendent's job was a reminder of a crucial reason the challenges of college refereeing seemed more interesting, and perhaps more instructive, than that of the pros. The NBA is show business, and nobody needs to hide that fact. College sports, however, are compelled to perform a different dance. NCAA athletes are enrolled as college students. The coaches are employees of the schools, even if they don't always seem to know it. Colleges and universities, as a matter of institutional pride, avowedly champion the principle of ethical behavior. They punish cheating. They proclaim a commitment to the implementation of a "level playing field." Fairness, as a concept, undergirds their very identity.

When I watch a pro game, I understand, and accept, that it was played for tangible, material rewards, and that the "true spirit of competition" so prized by commentators is an ancillary feature, and largely irrelevant to the outcome. And that coveted outcome, as the great Vince Lombardi always reminded, cannot be ambiguous. "If it doesn't matter who wins or loses," he famously said, "then why do we bother keeping score?"

Another telling difference between pro and college officials is that NBA refs are full-time professionals whereas college refs, for the most part, are not.

Many college conferences have traditionally had a stated preference to hire officials who enjoyed another source of income, a traditional "day job." Refs who did not exclusively depend on their game-day paychecks were valued as freelancers in the original meaning of the term; if they were not financially dependent on the gig, they would be freer to decide what was right without fear of reprisal.

Another reason the college leagues preferred referees with "day jobs" was, quite bluntly, a perception that men of more well-rounded interests would best represent the sport. Referees who'd achieved standing in the vocational world apart from basketball were considered more likely to be the type of upstanding citizens — reliable, organized, collaborative, sociable — in whom we'd entrust this precious, albeit undervalued, task of determining fairness on the court. Put another way: a guy who loves the sport, is struggling to find his niche (maybe an ex-player hoping to reconnect with bygone glories), and needs the paycheck, was not the ideal profile that the administrators desired for the men in zebra shirts.

Pro refs are full-time employees of the NBA, with benefits. They work a season that extends roughly October through early June. College refs are independent contractors with no benefits. They are free to make their own arrangements with the various leagues that might provide them with work. They work November through late March. Some work infrequently, a couple dozen games per year or fewer; others work almost ceaselessly during the heart of the season, ninety games or more squeezed into five months. The ranks of college refs currently include a psychologist, police sharpshooter, agronomy researcher, legislative aide, numerous small businessmen, attorneys, contractors, realtors, teachers of nearly every subject and every grade level, corporate executives, nonprofit administrators, municipal officials, facility managers, sales managers, and sales reps of every stripe.

As the pay has increased (compensation can be as much as $2,500 per game in the major conferences), and the added TV exposure has enhanced the allure, more referees have sought to make officiating their full-time livelihood. But for the time being, officiating remains, for most, a sideline. It may amount to the most noteworthy activity in their lives. It may be the centerpiece of most of their social interactions ("What's Calipari really like?" "What d'ya think about that lockout of NFL refs?" "Which school's fans are the craziest?") But it does not fully define who they are professionally or what they do. It was at first surprising for me to learn that the college refs were moonlighting, but I've now come to see it as of a piece with their greater separateness, their otherness, their semi-alienated relationship to the sport they love.

Having referees with outside vocations also serves to nicely augment the NCAA's fondest wish that the competition be viewed as a purely amateur, love-of-the-sport exercise. Refs who hold straightforward jobs in ordinary communities serve to reinforce the impression of a sport overseen by high-minded volunteers, like neighborhood Little Leagues run by conscientious parents. NCAA basketball strives to polish its reputation as an amateur sport and is keen to capitalize on it. The myriad contradictions that imperil this image (for example, the NCAA recently signed a $10.8 billion, fourteen-year TV rights deal to the March Madness tournament) are glaring, and revolve around one screaming contradiction: this is megabucks entertainment that derives its immense popularity, and thus its huge commercial value, from a cozy affiliation with nonprofit institutions dedicated to higher learning.

Enter the ref. He stands dead center in that snarled intersection between the pursuit of victory and the principle of fairness. But the referee's value to the enterprise extends beyond mere enforcement of the rules. His presence is tantamount to a seal of legitimacy, a certification by qualified experts that the contest will be fair. This is comparable, for good and for ill, with what the credit-rating agencies like Dun & Bradstreet are supposed to provide for financial investors. *Our team of highly trained experts have looked this situation over pretty darn carefully and, frankly, it all looks on the up and up. We give this baby a triple-A.*

Why does this matter? Because a fans' affection for the game hinges on truly believing, or being plausibly able to convince himself, that both teams have a perfectly fair chance to win, that the "playing field" is "level." If fans have the slightest reason to suspect unfairness, or worse, a fix, the spectator experience becomes a lot less compelling. (And let's not even talk about the disruptive effect on the enterprise of gambling, since it's such a messy subject, that would result from widespread doubt about officiating competence or impartiality; the $12 billion that Bloomberg estimates is wagered on the annual March Madness tournament is, after all, supposed to be extraneous to the discussion of college sports.)

Fairness, moreover, is vital to the essential beauty of sports. Without the seal of legitimacy imparted by qualified referees, the fiercely contested games we've come so passionately to enjoy run the risk of being perceived as something not quite so noble. (Think of a presidential election, in some country we won't call our own, minus poll watchers and a verifiable vote count.) Without our complete faith that the contest is conducted with maximum attention to keeping it fair, it could be mistaken for a mere diversion, just another form of entertainment.

And *entertainment* is decidedly not how organized sports views itself or wants to promote itself. "Sports, capital S, and Entertainment, capital E, are not the same," wrote *Boston Globe* sports columnist and ESPN contributor Bob Ryan. "Repeat, n-o-t, the same. They may share certain characteristics, but they are not the same."

The special appeal of sports is that they are perceived as *more real*, that is, more urgent, and thus more exciting, than commercialized diversions. They are live! Fortunes are in the balance. At the moment of tip-off, who wins and who loses is deliciously unknowable. Referees are the glue that holds this package together. As with most complex, high-budget constructions, it's best if the glue is not visible.

"Sports has an end purpose beyond putting on a great show. . . . The object of all major sports competitions is to win," Ryan continued in the same column. "Concurrent with that goal is the concept of Justice."

Absent the guarantee that every effort has been expended to keep the competition fair, fans might as well turn to staged events like those of the Harlem Globetrotters, internationally acclaimed ambassadors of basketball. The Globetrotters put on a dazzling performance featuring marvelously talented athletes.

But there's a reason Globetrotter games are rarely prime time. Everybody knows that what the team is primarily doing is putting on a show. And everybody knows who's going to win.

These ruminations were running through my mind as I approached my first meeting with Hightower. They were, admittedly, the idle conjectures of a lifelong fan with a penchant for meandering into the less highlighted nooks and crannies of the sports experience.

Hightower, I quickly discovered, was far too absorbed by more pressing matters to spend time indulging my idle conjectures. I, after all, was a fan. He was a man in the trenches.

On those snarling, self-important coaches that seemed to me the very symbol of something gone wrong in the culture of college sports, Hightower asserted, "Those coaches are out there fighting for their career. They're under tremendous pressure. It's an emotional game. I understand that coaches are not just going to sit there and watch."

On the recruiting scandals and academic cover-up allegations besmirching college sports, Hightower demurred, "As an educator, I wonder if we are preparing these kids the right way. Outstanding athletes are so coddled by our society from an early age that their problems are already set by the time they get to college."

On dealing with rabid home-team fans, those frothing icons of the impossibly polarized point of view, "You can't get emotional when everyone else is screaming. You know it when you've missed a call. You can't overreact. The worst thing you can do is to go into a shell or try to make it up."

At one point, to illustrate the complexity of determining fouls that take place down low in the post, Hightower instructed me to stand up and position myself as though I was defending him. He, the offensive player, tried to back me closer to the hoop. We were on his plush burgundy and taupe carpet, situated between his desk and the bookshelf. From that framed photo on his wall, I could almost feel the spirit of Bobby Knight bemusedly stroking his chin, waiting to see what happened next.

What happened next was that Hightower, bigger, stronger, smarter, more experienced, more agile, far more savvy (and far better dressed), arched his torso slightly backward, nudged me with a lowered shoulder, abruptly shifted his weight, did something with his off-arm that I couldn't exactly account for except that it had the net effect of shuffling me backward and bringing him two feet nearer to the imaginary hoop.

"Was that a foul?" he asked me.

Which? The shoulder bump? The forearm jujitsu? I had no idea. But I was glad that someone did.

I'd entered a land of small mysteries and it struck me that Ed Hightower, educator and referee, would have a particularly excellent and possibly revealing courtside perspective on all of this — on basketball, on competition, on college sports in America, and on the struggle to achieve fairness in this hypercompetitive arena where both sides are angling for any kind of an edge. He would know, it seemed to me, a few things about the cost of "win at all costs."

One of the first things Hightower said to me, in the quaint grandeur of his high-ceilinged office, was that his job as superintendent of schools had much in common with the job of officiating college basketball. "As a superintendent I can never please everyone. My goal is to be fair and balanced. As superintendent, I make thousands of decisions that are going to be challenged by someone. Every day I make decisions that someone is going to disagree with. But somebody has to be in charge. It's the same on the court. The basketball arena is a very, very partisan place. If fair and balanced is my goal, what are the chances of pleasing all 16,000 people?"

WORST F**KING REF IN THE WORLD!

Early on a Saturday morning in January 2013, I joined Hightower at the Chicago O'Hare Marriott for a drive he would be taking that day to Madison, Wisconsin, along with Bo Boroski, his ref partner for an afternoon showdown between Big Ten rivals Illinois and Wisconsin.

During the winter months, the softly lit Marriott lobby and adjoining restaurant function for NCAA refs as a desert oasis watering hole would for nomadic Arab tribes. A dozen referees, all having flown in the night before, mingled at the bustling self-serve breakfast cafeteria, loading up on waffles and sausage and eggs before dispersing to their respective assignments in South Bend, Evanston, Milwaukee, Muncie, Champaign-Urbana, Peoria. Dressed in country club casual, pressed slacks, polished leather shoes, and pullover sweaters, they bantered with the familiarity of fraternity brothers reuniting after a few months apart. Which is more or less what they were.

Each game features a different configuration of officials. In this respect the refs are like skilled studio musicians brought together for a recording session. They're pros. They know what's expected. They'll have no trouble playing together. They've bonded in the unforgiving glare of center court while being showered with angry accusations. They've slogged hard highway miles under deadline pressure in thunderstorms and icy roads. They've attended charity events together and played golf with each other in the off-season.

They've annually participated in mandatory two-day preseason workshops that function like corporate executive retreats (though generally not held in opulent tax-haven vacation spas). They've swapped confidences about their personal lives (whose son is getting an MBA, whose wife had surgery, whose divorce is proving not as streamlined as hoped for) that are typically the province of blood relatives or close friends. In many cases, the comradely respect they've shared during the season has spilled over to satisfying friendships that are among the best they've ever enjoyed. The Final Four, at least for those like Hightower who'd been selected for it so often, could often feel like a family reunion, with spouses and children tagging along to enjoy the multiday festivities along with the families of other refs.

At the Marriott restaurant, sipping steaming coffee and gabbing, then pushing back from their plates and stretching their legs for the drive ahead, this clutch of refs could be mistaken for a corporate sales force winding up a training session before heading out to the territories. They exuded that kind of brightness about the challenges ahead.

Hightower alone wore a starched dress shirt and suit coat. He was every bit as jovial and wisecracking as his fraternity brothers and the relative refinement of his attire did not appear to separate him in any other way. Jesting and quipping, he gave as good as he got (about a flat tire en route to a big game in Bloomington, a shanked tee shot at a golf outing during the Maui Thanksgiving tournament) when it came to the gentle ribbing that's a constant when referees gather. His voice has a deep natural boom and he speaks with a crisply enunciated ardor that listeners experience viscerally, almost as sound waves. As befits a man who's made his share of announcements over a scratchy public address system, he hardly says anything without a sharp emphasis of each syllable. Temperamentally, he's an enthusiast, a fervent champion of the "be all you can be" approach to life. "You've got it!" he is prone to crow whenever he agrees with something you've said, and he has a way of conveying this with such vigor that one can be fooled into thinking maybe you really do "have it."

On the way out to the parking lot, Hightower and Boroski, partners for the day, wheeled nearly identical black suitcases. Boroski, a thoughtful former college baseball pitcher who once harbored big league dreams, had flown to Chicago from Tampa, where he'd worked a Big East game, and tomorrow he would head to Columbus to do Michigan–Ohio State. Hightower's schedule had been lighter, having worked only the Nebraska-Michigan game earlier in the week. But at his superintendent's job the pressures had mounted in the wake of the recent Newtown, Connecticut, school massacre. This coming Monday he would preside over a community meeting on the subject of school safety. "We are going to discuss school safety," is how he intended to open the meeting. "But we are *not* going to discuss gun rights. And we *not* going to discuss the Second Amendment."

An early January drive from Chicago to Madison can be a winter highway nightmare. Like long-distance truckers, every ref has his horror tales of nail-biting journeys through blinding blizzards and perilous sleet. Referees are required to be at the arena two hours before game time.

This morning had started out drizzly but it was already clearing and the temperature was starting to plummet. Not a problem. Frigid air with no precipitation was, given the alternative, almost ideal weather conditions. Hightower figured he'd made this exact drive, O'Hare to the Kohl Center (or its predecessor, the Wisconsin Field House) as many as fifty times. He knew the route like a seasoned commuter, which exit to take off I-94 and on to the Madison back roads into the Kohl's service entrance. He had the same level of familiarity with the long drives from Edwardsville to Bloomington, Edwardsville to Champaign-Urbana, Chicago to Lafayette, Indiana, and from the Detroit airport to East Lansing and Ann Arbor. Boroski, younger and with fewer games under his belt, had nonetheless done the O'Hare to Madison trip many times and took the wheel of the late-model Hertz sedan. He was a quick study. This trip would be a glide.

"Glide," on second thought, might not be the most apt description. Referees drive fast. I'd like to report they only drive as fast as state law allows, but that would be a bit of a cover-up. Refs speeding along the interstate to a game are rarely passed by other vehicles. They tailgate almost compulsively. They steer with their knees in the fast lane while grabbing for fries in the Burger King bag wedged by the door. On the highways they are agile, daring, fearless, cocky, opportunistic drivers. When I pointed this out, and not approvingly, to Hightower and other refs, they invariably claimed that so-and-so (the name Jim Burr came up a lot) was worse. Just like those shoulder-shrugging, hey-I-didn't-do-nothing young dudes accusing the opposing player of having deliberately initiated the contact.

Wisconsin's cavernous, 17,000 seat Kohl Center on this clear, cold January Saturday was packed with high-spirited Badger basketball fans. The arena, named after the former U.S. senator Herb Kohl and financed largely by a generous $25 million donation from his family business, was one of those gleaming glass-and-steel university sports facilities whose improbable grandeur, set on a college campus, immediately lets you know there's more than fun and games (and education) going on here. The arena's thirty-six luxury suites, terrazzo flooring on the concourse and washrooms, and integrated video, scoring, advertising, and display system, otherwise known as a scoreboard, rivaled the lavishness of most professional arenas, including that of the nearby NBA franchise, the Milwaukee Bucs, not coincidentally owned by Herb Kohl.

Midway into the second half, the game had already reached blowout proportions. Underdog Wisconsin was leading Illinois, the tenth-ranked team in the country that week, by a lopsided score of 54–26. Seated beside me in the lower loge, section 104, were three congenial, middle-aged gentlemen with jumbo bratwursts and popcorn and beers perched precariously on their laps. In keeping with the hyper-partisan spirit of the event, each wore a bright red sweater. The "Grateful Red" is how the more rabid student section liked to refer to itself. Although unabashed in their sympathies, these fellows were fairly subdued and for good reason. Nearly every play, every shot, every rebound, every loose ball was going Wisconsin's way.

Until this point, I'd paid scant attention to these men except to note, with a slight tinge of envy, how comfortably planted they seemed in this place, and how at-ease they were in each others' company. Clearly they were good buddies, familiar and convivial. I figured them to be alumni, their friendship going back to UW undergraduate days when they were just starting out in life, football at Camp Randall, hanging at the Rat, Saturday nights cruising State Street, caffeinated all-nighters during finals. And what better way to reconvene in adulthood than huddling inside the warmth of the cavernous Kohl Center for an afternoon of Big Ten basketball action?

Outside, the north wind was blasting across the glistening frozen lake. Inside, it was all merriment for the Badger faithful. Their three-point shots were falling. When they missed, they grabbed their own rebound, glanced at the coach for instruction, and reset the offense. The fellows seated beside me, good-naturedly talking all the while, seemed to be paying less and less attention to the game. I caught a scrap of conversation about one of their daughters applying to law school. Another had an unemployed son living at home but wasn't annoyed about it — yet. Such relaxed ebb and flow of fraternal banter is an essential if overlooked part of the sports fan's pleasure. Watching an athletic contest seemed, for these guys, to be mostly an excuse to gather together and seamlessly free associate across a broad range of topics including, from time to time, the game at hand.

Down on the glimmering court, Wisconsin worked the ball around the horn for a shot. It clanged and the long rebound was batted among flailing hands before skittering toward the sideline. Badger guard Traevon Jackson, son of Jimmy Jackson, the legendary Ohio State and NBA star, and currently a Big Ten announcer, hustling as if the game were tied, dove after the ball and wound up crashing into the Illinois forward who'd arrived there first.

Hightower, in the trail position, was appropriately near to the action and had a clear view. The shrill tweet of his whistle halted play. His arms shot forward, hands thrust up: the signal for a pushing violation. The foul was an obvious call — or so one would think.

Suddenly the amiable guy directly beside me lowered the red-and-white popcorn box from his face and bellowed with a rage that could only be characterized as demented, "Hightower, you suck!"

The Badgers had victory locked up. The foul that Hightower had called was not even remotely disputable, not by Jackson, not by his teammates, not by his ever-vigilant and crafty coach, Bo Ryan, not by Ryan's bevy of assistant coaches, not, I would bet, by Jackson's own mother if she were watching. But this otherwise mild-mannered fan had seen something he did not like, something that launched him out of his genial torpor, and he yelled again, "You suck, Hightower!"

I had to wonder what this guy's response might be if the foul in question had been even marginally disputable? Or the contest had been even remotely close? If the clock had been ticking down, and the game was one that truly mattered? What if the call had been made on the final shot, with a one-point spread, in the NCAA tournament? What kind of invective would spew forth in reaction to a crunch time call that went the wrong way?

On the face of it, an NCAA basketball referee would seem to be exactly the kind of noble figure, the solitary fearless sheriff laying down the law in lawless Tombstone that Americans normally admire. Framed this way, as a throwback to frontier justice, standing tall for what is right and isolated by the very nature of his mission, the lone referee is straight out of a cowboy saga, high noon at half court. We townsfolk in the grandstand should be grateful to have someone (not us) take on this vital yet thankless task.

Yet the relative anonymity of the refs certainly makes them easier to scorn and, ironically, renders the few who do achieve some prominence, like Hightower, ripe for even greater abuse. Fans don't especially want to know much about refs and their particular biographical profiles, especially about a man like Hightower, whose professional responsibilities could be considered at least as substantial as those of any men's basketball coach. Fans don't really care to know that every call a ref makes is graded and assessed after every game, that the refs who work elite tournaments are selected on the basis of superior performance during the regular season, or that — and here's the really big one — they genuinely do not care who wins or losses.

Simply put, refs are the antithesis of fans. Immersed in the action, arguably in possession of the best vantage points in the house, they remain unconcerned with the stated objective of the entire event, namely to determine a winner. This blithe disregard for the ultimate outcome, nearly Buddhist in its remove from worldly concerns, is especially confounding to fans.

I once questioned Hightower on this assertion that referees do not, in fact, care which team wins. He insisted that this was indeed true, at least in the conventional way that fans come to a game with a preconceived desire to see a specific team, *their* team, triumph. Refs, he acknowledged, do periodically come to care about the outcome; they are, after all, only human. But when a ref is pleased by an outcome it is for fundamentally different reasons. "Yes, you sometimes care who wins," Hightower confided. "You give both teams an opportunity to win, by being fair, by being objective out there. You've done your job well. So when the team that's played best wins the game that night, yes, you're happy that they won."

Branded by their zebra shirts, they are isolated. Their every action, and every inaction is witnessed by as many as 30,000 unforgiving critics in some arenas, plus countless millions more watching on television, some of whom may indeed enjoy a better angle on a particular play, or at least think they do. The vast increase in the number of games telecast as the result of the NCAA's industriousness — ESPN broadcast well over 1,100 games in 2012–13, compared to 281 in 1996 — and the rampant increase in new media mechanisms for accessing and sharing video, places refs in an unrelenting spotlight. There is nowhere to run, nowhere to hide, no help in sight, and no hope of appeal.

"Media scrutiny today is ramped by a thousand percent," observed former referee Hank Nichols, who fondly recalls the days when a referee's performance needed only to meet the approval of two demanding coaches, ten self-centered athletes, and 10,000 to 15,000 thousand myopic fans.

The average viewership from the combined network telecasts for each game in the 2013 March Madness tournament was 10.2 million people, and that figure rose to a whopping 23.4 million for the championship game. It's no revelation that college basketball has become big business. It's compulsively expansionist and, like any enterprise with wind in its sails and ample financing, it is constantly pursuing imaginative ways to further market the product. Network broadcasts today rarely take a night off during the season, and there are many stretches in the schedule ("Feast Week" during Thanksgiving break, "Holiday Hoops" during Christmas–New Year's, league tournament time, NCAA tournament time) when live action on TV can be viewed nonstop from lunchtime until late into the night.

ESPN has shrewdly packaged games to make certain that no day of the week is without substantial opportunity for spectators. "Big Monday" features back-to-back games from the Big East and Big Twelve; "Super Tuesday," the Big Ten and SEC; "Wednesday Night Hoops," the ACC plus all of the above; "Thursday Night Showcase" consists of five games from across the land. Fridays have become functionally like the Sabbath with a slightly reduced emphasis (nationally, that is). Weekends are busy, busy, busy. On top of all that, ESPN in cooperation with the NCAA has conjured an assortment of made-for-TV attractions, including Jimmy V Week, the Old Spice Classic, "BracketBusters," in which mid-major teams hoping to make it into the NCAA tournament do battle in late February, and "Rivalry Week" pairing traditional foes like Indiana versus Purdue.

And if the games themselves should falter in their ability to deliver high drama sufficient to keep viewers watching, there's always a useful villain waiting conveniently in the wings.

A survey of the torrent of expressed opinions posted by college basketball fans (reviewing these is not an exercise recommended for the time-constrained or the squeamish) reveals there are literally dozens of refs working Division 1 men's basketball who have been castigated as "the worst f**king ref ever!" Indeed, it appears that the only way for a ref to avoid this label is to be too inexperienced or too obscure. The list includes, perhaps not coincidentally, many who are otherwise recognized as the most skilled and accomplished, including Jim Burr, Karl Hess, Mike Sanzere, Tim Higgins, Jamie Luckie, Pat Driscoll, Ted Valentine, and Tony Greene, who had the distinction of being the focus of a blog exclusively devoted to his alleged malfeasance. "Istonygreeneonthetake" consisted of dozens of posts spanning several seasons in which the kindest thing ever said was, "Tony Greene's officiating not suspicious in this one." (Greene, a project manager for the Georgia Department of Economic Development, has reffed five NCAA finals. "All a part of the job," was his take on the vitriolic attacks.)

Ridicule comes with the territory, and college basketball's maniacal fan base of passionate home-team loyalists is notoriously easy to provoke. Still, it's worth noting that Ed Hightower has perhaps been more widely, vividly, heatedly, and imaginatively pilloried than any ref in college basketball history. While that dubious status is partly a function of the sheer volume of games he'd been part of during a three-decade career, along with the prestige of those games (countless times on national television, twelve times officiating the Final Four, four times reffing the NCAA championship game), it was also a function of a weird fetish for vilification that's caught on with fans.

Mocking Hightower through Photoshop manipulation had became a bizarre hobby on sports sites and blogs where, in his zebra shirt, whistle dangling, arm thrust upward for an emphatic call, one can view him straddling a rocket that's blasting off, leaping onto Oprah's sofa to make a call, whistling Jesus for a traveling violation as He walks across the water, riding a giraffe bareback, cavorting onstage with the Village People, on roller skates leading the pack in a roller derby, helping Mel Gibson lead the charge in *Braveheart*, lolling on the verdant river bank in the painting *Sunday Afternoon on the Island of La Grande Jatte*, superimposed onto the

Loraine Motel balcony in the famous photo where Martin Luther King lay dying.

Twitter and fan sites are hardly models of decorum, yet still: "I hope Ed Hightower croaks after this game." "Ed Hightower again? Why do we always get this clown?" "Just saw on Twitter that Hightower's refereeing the game tonight. This team can't catch a break." "Ten Things the Big 10 Should Do Before It Expands. #1 Put Ed Hightower on a one-way rocket to the sun." "I promised you'd we'd be ever vigilant at All Along Ed's Watchtower, where bad officiating is our business." "One Fan's Plea That NCAA Referee Ed Hightower Must Go" (title of article on BleacherReport.com)

What's all that about?

A stranger to our shores, uninitiated in the habits of our sports culture, might be forgiven for assuming that spectators to an amateur athletic contest between institutions devoted to higher education would demonstrate a kinder approach to partisanship than, say, European soccer hooligans. But that's an assumption only a stranger would make. Officiating miscues, whether real or perceived, are savored by sports fans, and never more so than when the game turns sour. Ripping the ref has become something like an entitlement of the fan experience. It's as if no game is complete without it.

As it turned out, the Badger fan hollering out "Hightower, you suck" that frigid Saturday in Madison quickly simmered down and resumed amiably chatting with his buddies. Pretending that I'd missed the disputed sequence, I politely inquired what exactly had so disturbed him about the call Hightower had made. The fellow just smiled. He wasn't about to defend or explain the outburst. With a swig of beer and a no-big-deal shoulder shrug, he let me know that whatever it had been, he sure wasn't about to let it ruin his afternoon.

The game having long since ceased to be competitive and with time quickly running out, this mild-mannered Badger fan had merely wanted his money's worth.

. . .

True officiating travesties, as opposed to the invented or imagined ones, are red meat to ravenous fans. Fortunately for the protein-hungry, each season reliably produces a handful of blown calls and glaring doozies that invariably provide plenty to chew on.

One that makes everyone's "Ten Worst" list, for those who keep such lists, is the 2011 Big East tournament game between Rutgers and St. John's. It would possibly be considered the very worst ever, had the stakes been slightly higher, had it been, say, a late round NCAA tournament game.

Down 65–63 with 4.9 seconds left, Rutgers lobbed a long in-bounds pass that was intercepted by a St. John's defender who took a couple of quick dribbles to free himself from traffic and then, thinking the game was over (it was not), picked up his dribble and sprinted with the ball along the sideline, apparently in celebration, stepping out-of-bounds and flinging the ball into the stands—all before time expired. Despite numerous clear infractions—traveling, out-of-bounds, delay of game for tossing the ball away—the refs held their whistles. The lead official declared the game over, walking off the court. The other two refs ignored Rutgers' desperate pleas.

Nearly two years after the game, comments were still being posted at the YouTube site displaying the sequence: "It shows there is a shortage in good officials." "I don't even know the rules and I know that's a travel." "That shit needs to be retracted or the officials fired for that crap!!"

On January 1, 2013, in the opening game of the Big East season, Marquette's Junior Cadougan drained a long three-pointer at the end of regulation time to tie UConn. When the teams reassembled to start the overtime, UConn's Shabazz Napier controlled the ball off the tip and drove to the hoop. A leaping Marquette player swatted the shot away in what was clearly a case of goaltending. The whistle was blown. The bucket awarded to UConn.

Okay so far. Except, well, except for the fact that at the start of the overtime each team had mistakenly lined up facing the wrong end of the court. Realizing this only after the goaltending call was made, the refs hastily conferred. It's safe to say none had ever confronted this predicament before. More or less winging it, the refs opted to nullify the basket that had been awarded to UConn, reasoning that it was technically not possible to goaltend at your own basket which, in retrospect, had been exactly the case.

The officials, it turned out, were wrong. The rulebook (Rule 5, Section 1, Article 3) states, in essence, that play should have resumed with the teams heading in the *right* direction, but any play that occurred *before* the discovery should be counted. Marquette went on to win by six points.

Wrote Troy Machir on NBCSports.com, "We witnessed something last night that I am certain I have never witnessed at the Division-I level. Thank you Big East referees, for making sure we learn something new every day."

Referee Karl Hess admitted the error and apologized. UConn coach Kevin Ollie graciously said the blown call was not the reason his squad lost.

Some fans were less forgiving.

"Hess is a protected figure (IMO) just like any other pro-Carolina goon in this scandal of theirs. He is compiling a resume that should at least get him demoted to a lower division or high school officiating," one fan posted on the Mbd.Scout.com site after the game.

"How many times does Karl Hess have to screw up before someone raises a protest?" wrote another.

ating questions are to be filtered off-site through the coordinator of officials, John Adams.

The besieged ref is thus often left in the position of a defendant whose lawyer forbids him to take the stand. In the seething court of public opinion, the refs have no advocates and most have learned that the less said the better. For my interviews, Hightower sought and received permission from the Big Ten. Many refs I spoke with and found to be insightful, articulate, and worthy of quoting at length do not appear by name in this book. That was not due to a fetish for anonymity.

It makes for an odd imbalance, this mandatory silence imposed on the accused. There's no cheering to counteract the condemnation, no kudos as counterweight to the opprobrium. The refs' only consolation is the personal satisfaction that comes from getting it right under tough conditions. Like performing artists, they know in their gut when they've nailed it, even if we do not.

. . .

Morgantown, West Virginia, Saturday afternoon, January 26, 2008. The West Virginia University Mountaineers were hosting their archrival, the Hoyas of Georgetown University. Sporting events in Morgantown, like those in many college towns far from metropolitan cultural centers, enjoy a special prominence. With over 15,000 fans attending the game (in a community with a total population of less than 30,000) on a dank overcast day, the Georgetown game was the biggest show in town, and certainly the only one capable of drawing network television coverage. For a few fleeting hours, Morgantown was not just another burg in the rolling Appalachian hills, but a bona fide center of attention.

The score was 57–56 in favor of Georgetown with six seconds left in the second half. West Virginia was about to take the ball out from the baseline behind its own basket.

"Six seconds left now," purred ESPN's Dave Pasch with the kind of understated confidence that announcers adopt when the unfolding drama requires no further huffing and puffing. "What is West Virginia going to do?"

The two head coaches prowling the sidelines were not exactly pictures of calm. West Virginia's coach was the hulking Bob Huggins. He was known as "Huggy Bear" but not because he exuded childlike lovability. Following sixteen years as head coach at University of Cincinnati, where he enjoyed considerable success (399 wins, 127 losses) as well as generating substantial criticism (a paltry 30 percent player graduation rate, too many appearances by players on local police blotters), this season marked his return to the WVU campus where he'd been a standout varsity player more than thirty years before. Huggins wanted this game. Like most coaches, he wanted every game.

Huggins' counterpart, Georgetown coach John Thompson III, was a more modestly sized version of his legendary predecessor as Georgetown coach, his father John Thompson II. Coincidentally, Patrick Ewing Jr., the son of the Georgetown star of yore most responsible for the school's eminence in basketball, was playing forward in this game. Like his coach in relationship to his famous father, Ewing Jr. was a more moderately sized and less capable version of the old man. The Hoyas were ranked no. 9 in the country. A road win under pressure in an arena as unrelentingly hostile as the Coliseum would be exactly the type of character-building confidence boost that coaches crave for their squads as they look ahead to March Madness.

With six seconds left, WVU was down a point as they passed the ball in from behind their basket. Coaches know only too well how many things can go wrong in these precious waning seconds. Based on too many experiences, they know that the referee, who everyone would prefer to be invisible, can in these final frantic moments suddenly rise up and roar. Nobody wants that to happen, least of all the referee.

West Virginia's inbounds pass went to point guard Darris Nichols. He dribbled at a sprint up the left side in a play diagrammed by Huggins during the frenzied time-out. Six seconds is not long, but with athletes this quick, it was enough time for one well-crafted offensive attempt. An open shot from the key, perhaps, coming off a screen, or better yet, a drive to the hoop that carried the added benefit of potentially drawing a foul. Or the illusion of a foul.

And that's precisely the play Huggins designed. Crossing half-court Nichols zipped a bullet pass to Da'Sean Butler, the talented 6' 7" sophomore who would go on to play in the NBA. Butler took the pass on the left baseline, far from the basket. There were fewer than four seconds left. He did not hesitate. He dribbled once with his left hand, took one gazelle stride and bounded upward, swooping toward the hoop. Somehow, he had found a seam in the defense (coach Thompson would doubtless have harsh words with his team later about that lapse) and for an instant Butler looked to be soaring high enough, and near enough, to jam the ball through. But he was not quite there, and chose instead to float the ball up with a gentle, deft scoop. He accomplished this with a magisterial grace, as so many of these wonderful young athletes manage to do. Clearly this was a move he'd rehearsed, soaring toward the hoop and delicately flipping the ball into a perfect petite arc.

But at the last possible instant before Butler's adroit little floater could descend through the net, Georgetown's Ewing, with a catlike quickness to perfectly match Butler's, flashed down the lane. With impeccable choreographer's timing, Ewing rose just behind the lift of the ball as it floated rim-ward, and swatted it away triumphantly. Game over. Georgetown wins. No joy in Mudville. ("'Kill the umpire,' shouted someone in the stand," goes one line from the famous poem. "And it's likely they'd have killed him had not Casey raised his hand.")

Ah, but not so fast. Huggins, showing some of his old athleticism, stormed onto the court as though shot from a cannon. His dark suit coat, baggy to begin with, flapped about as he hurtled toward center court, his right arm vigorously chopping like a woodsman hacking a tree limb. Huggins was demanding a call of goaltending (the official hand signal for this infraction is a more civilized version of Huggins's tomahawk chop). If a defensive player rises up and interferes with a shot once its arc has reached its apex and the ball has begun its descent, this illegality is termed "goaltending," and a college basketball league that failed to police it properly would be one sorry mess. Huggins wanted the Ewing block nullified and he had no doubt who was responsible for making that call.

Ed Hightower and Pat Driscoll were the refs best able to observe what was taking place. Hightower was stationed just beyond the arc. Of the three officials on the court, he likely had the best view of the last play. It was significant that he did not blow his whistle, and did not lift his arm. The analogy between basketball officiating and a courtroom judge presiding at trial is questionable and only occasionally illuminating (more on this later). But we'll try it out here: Huggins at this moment was protesting as though he believed the judge was napping during closing arguments.

Goaltending, according to Hightower, is the single most difficult call to make. Unlike other violations that appear imprecise yet demand precise judgments — charging, for example — goaltending always, *always*, results in a two-point swing. Making the call awards the basket; declining to make it upholds the legitimacy of the defensive maneuver that prevented the shot from going in. Moreover, the judgment needed to ascertain goaltending involves all the troublesome components that make basketball officiating so vexing: frantic action, vantage-point limitations, squishiness in the rule, and an ironclad obligation to render a binding and instantaneous verdict. Even if the verdict is to make no call at all.

Hightower strode calmly, determinedly off the court. Huggins stalked him every menacing inch of the way, bellowing and gesticulating. Hightower was several inches shorter than Huggins, and older by a decade. He continued to walk proudly, eyes straight ahead. His objective was to get off the court and out of the spotlight, and he was not going to be detained. Huggins tried to impede Hightower's retreat by what might plausibly be considered peaceful means, moving alongside step-by-step in such proximity that Hightower could not walk a straight path off the court without knocking knees. But physical contact would be a gross error with significant consequence, and Huggins knew not to push this strategy too far.

The crowd followed Huggins as he tracked Hightower. The coach's determination to seek redress seemed to give them hope and the Mountaineer fans, fingers crossed, watched this final pantomime play out, Huggins ranting, Hightower retreating, the weary players milling about. Might a reversal of fortune yet be salvaged? If sports were in fact purely a theatrical performance, highly improvised yet nonetheless delivered with artistic aims, we would know that the purpose of this pas de deux was textbook stagecraft, a dénouement devised to allow the audience to blow off steam and regain equilibrium before getting on with its life.

Hightower kept walking, eyes unwaveringly forward. Huggins stayed with him every step, strenuously pleading a case that had already been settled. When Hightower crossed the baseline, veering toward the ramp leading to the locker room, and finally disappeared from view, the moment had that pro forma finality you get at rock concerts when, after the last encore has left the audience shrieking, the management-controlled houselights pop on to signal in no uncertain terms that it's time to quit shouting for more, and start heading home.

Game over.

Video of the final play was posted online soon afterward. The heated observations, some wise, some blathering, some shrewd, some imbecilic, seven pages of commentary alone on the YouTube link displaying the replay, underscored one of the little-acknowledged (and lesser-understood) by-products of our modern-day 24/7 sports culture: there's a multitude of people out there who should maybe find more productive outlets for their considerable analytical acumen.

I've always said that borderline goaltends should not be called. This block was close enough to stand.

You need to open those eyes! definitely goaltending! don't matter, revenge was served tonight!

No, we have eyes, if you think that's not goaltending . . . you are a blind asshole!

Goaltending. It was barely going down. They could've at least reviewed it instead of running away from Bob Huggins.

From courtside in Morgantown, as the stadium gradually emptied of despondent fans, Len Elmore, the ESPN color commentator who had been repeatedly reviewing the tape of the final play, opined, "It was difficult to tell. We've seen so many different angles. The ball [Butler's shot] has to be on its downward flight. If it reached its apex and took a dip, it was almost imperceptible. And the official has to make a split-second call. We [the announcers and viewers] have the benefit of slow motion. Maybe it might have dipped, maybe it didn't. The official out on top is the one responsible for that call."

That "official on top" was Hightower.

One would think that a play like the Ewing block, with the outcome of the game hinging on one final judgment that only he, the referee, was in a position to make, would be Hightower's worst fear. It is not. Tough calls, judiciously rendered without flinching, without vacillation, without apologizing for his role as the one responsible for having to make the call before all the facts can possibly be gathered, before all the evidence can be processed and methodically assessed, was his point of pride, never more so than before a hostile crowd.

From that perspective, the Georgetown–West Virginia barn-burner, when all was said and done, felt pretty good.

Goal tend! This ball was on the way down. Why did the refs all sprint off the court?

Ed Hightower was also working the WVU-Oklahoma game that they played in Charleston. Towards the end of the game, he gave it to Oklahoma. There was an elbow to the face of Alex Ruoff that Hightower paid no attention to.

Ed Hightower is the worst official in the game of basketball.

COTTON FIELDS BACK HOME

Ed Hightower was born and raised in an isolated southern Missouri farming community that had far more in common with the agrarian nineteenth-century America of Mark Twain than the Internet Age that bestowed on him a qualified renown.

The Hightower family home in Gobler, Missouri, sat on a weedy patch of property set back from the Gobler Road, a hard dirt straightaway that ran due west from Deering, an equally isolated hamlet. The town of Gobler — it verged on hyperbole to even call it a town — was located in the very southeast corner of the state, in the finger of land that hangs down between Tennessee to the East and Arkansas to the west. It consisted of little more than a general store, a post office, and cluster of tin-roof homes that could probably best be described as shacks.

The family house was a four-room, tin-roofed wood structure that lacked indoor plumbing. It looked across a patchwork of cotton fields that stretched as far as the eye could see, which, given the unwavering flatness of the terrain, was very far indeed. The landscape in every direction displayed the same monotonous expanse, barren of trees, bushes, or anything taller than the cotton plant itself.

Hightower's antagonists up in the grandstands have often accused him of trying to control the game, of wanting to insinuate himself into the mix, of wanting to make *himself* the focal point. Every time he'd heard that accusation — and he couldn't help but occasionally hear it — it made Hightower laugh. Nothing could be farther from the truth. In his mind, the only basketball hoop he ever controlled, or wanted to, was the simple homemade construction, a steel rim bolted to a sturdy square of plywood, he'd built with his brothers in the yard beside his home in Gobler.

The backboard was attached to a tall pole. The pole was embedded in a deep hole dug in the ground and tightly packed with dirt. The height of the hoop was not precisely measured and probably fell short of the regulation ten feet. The so-called court was a hard earth surface that could be etched with the semblance of out-of-bounds lines to make play more interesting, more competitive, more like the real thing. Whatever that was. The family did not have a TV. Basketball, baseball, and football were games the kids played for fun. Sports were entertainment in the sense that they provided a free way to amuse oneself.

It was the mid-1960s. Then and now, this isolated agricultural region was an island in time that could easily serve, with little revision, as the setting for a movie depicting life in the rural south in the decades following — or even before — the Civil War. The roads are long and straight and dusty. Dwellings, in sore need of paint, are few and far between. The land extends without variation in every direction, like a great frozen lake. The soil is almost entirely given over to agricultural cultivation of beans, corn, molasses, and, most significantly, King Cotton. Situated in a flood plain between the Mississippi and St. Francis Rivers, the Bootheel region of Missouri was uninhabited swampland as recently as 1900. Around that time the swamps were systematically drained by commercial logging companies through the construction of an elaborate network of drainage ditches, diversion channels and levees. What remained, once all the trees were cleared, was some of the most fertile farmland in the United States. Almost everyone who lived in Gobler, or Deering, or Kennett, or Hayti, or other subsistence communities in Pemiscot County, drew their primary income from farming.

Presents were a rarity in the Hightower household. Cash was in short supply. Ed doesn't recall what he might have done to "deserve" a basketball rim or when it was purchased. Most likely it was viewed by his mother less as a present than a supplement to domestic life. That's the role sports played in their life, a terrific outlet for filling in idle time.

Ed knew next to nothing about the rules of basketball. He knew that he liked the game, the quick cuts, the emphasis on cleverness and deftness of movement, the handiwork involved in dribbling and the measured force needed to launch a shot that went far enough but not too far. Lacking a TV, he had no way of knowing how sophisticated the simple elements of this game could become when performed by brilliant athletes who devoted themselves to the task. He'd never seen a five-on-five full-court contest. He hardly knew the rules beyond the basics anyone could glean through common sense: you weren't allowed to push or shove (this wasn't football) and if someone did so deliberately, with the explicit aim of gaining an advantage, it was a clear violation and they should be told in no uncertain terms to cut it out.

The Hightower hoop when raised had the rough-hewn, improvised character of Naismith's infamous peach basket. The support pole was a bit wobbly. The backboard vibrated in a stiff wind. The rim slanted slightly downward. Yet for all its homemade imperfections, it was perfect for its purpose. In free time after school, after chores, after homework, after church, when weather and Mama permitted it, Ed would practice his shot. He had strong legs and a flair for launching the ball off his shoulder, his fingertips grazing its pebbled surface. Like many a child absorbed in the private satisfactions of repeating the component essentials, over and over, throwing, catching, kicking, batting, Ed's thoughts as he practiced darted and soared.

The ball would leave his hand and lift toward the rim. His imagination trailed the ball like the tail of a kite, up, up, then gracefully descending. Youngsters practicing basketball by themselves often reenact this timeless ritual, the gradual honing of a core athletic skill, as their imaginations, freed from earthly gravity, find footing and gather momentum and eventually take flight. Ed was no different. With churning legs, keeping his dribble low, he drove to the hoop, rising up for the shot, rising up to be somebody beyond who he was.

If he'd watched more sports on TV, if his upbringing had been more conventionally saturated with popular media, that "somebody" he sought to be would likely have been a very specific person, probably a sports star. Oscar Robertson and Lou Hudson were his favorites. But even to a child imitating, or trying to, the smooth release of a hero's jumper, such superstars were not quite the ubiquitous cultural figures they are today. They were known. They were widely admired. They functioned as models, in their moves, their style, their stats. And it was possible, of course, to dream of doing what they did, dazzling the opposition and making it all the way to the pros.

From Ed's fingertips, the ball took flight. As it rose toward the hoop, his vision of what lay ahead momentarily elevated with it. He did not know where or how, but he hoped to get a chance. And maybe, if he was feeling particularly giddy that day, if his chores were completed and his homework was done, and if the long outside shot he'd launched while he daydreamed looked to be on target and true, well, the crowd would go wild!

Hightower's mother, Daisy Laman, left Grenada, Mississippi, in 1946 where her family had lived since the days of slavery, and moved seventy-five miles north to Missouri.

It's easy to understand why an African American family would wish to abandon Grenada County in the middle of the twentieth century. The rural agricultural region, heart of cotton country, was home to some of the ugliest episodes of post–Civil War history. In the war, Missouri had been a "border state," that is, a slave state that chose not to secede. Mississippi had been the heart and soul of the Confederacy. It was a state whose laws had prohibited blacks from being jurors and where the crime of miscegenation was punishable by life in prison. Grenada's history of lynchings — there were four on the same day in 1885 — left a legacy of racist intimidation that may have diminished over the decades but remained current and alive.

For black families, life in Grenada was a nearly feudal condition, an improvement on abject slavery but a far cry from economic equality. Most black families lived in small shacks on back roads and worked as underpaid sharecroppers for white landowners. In the early 1960s, Mississippi was ground zero of the civil rights campaign in the south and yet even veteran organizers considered Grenada, in the words of Bruce Hartford, a Southern Christian Leadership Conference activist, "a tough nut to crack." As of 1966, only 3 percent of the eligible blacks were registered to vote in Grenada County.

Gobler, where Daisy Laman's family settled, was nearly identical to Grenada in many ways — rural and agrarian, hot and impossibly humid in the growing season, with an economy dependent on cotton, as well as soybeans, sweet corn, and field corn. And yet for all the similarities, Gobler was different in one most meaningful way. It promised, if only because it was not Mississippi, a marginally better chance. In Missouri, it was easier for African Americans to purchase land and climb the entrepreneurial ladder. Daisy's father owned over 100 acres. Her grandfather owned 180. Wes Miller, her uncle, became a field boss who contracted with farmers to supply workers. That was progress.

Ed's father, also named Edward but nicknamed "Rail," made an identical migration with his family, Grenada to Gobler, at roughly the same time. Throughout the early and mid-twentieth century, as cotton prices dropped and northern manufacturing began to boom, blacks fled the rural south, heading north to Chicago, Cleveland, St. Louis, Milwaukee, Detroit. This great migration to the industrial north was not, however, the course chosen by the Laman and Hightower families. Instead, they transplanted themselves a short distance upriver to reengage in the familiar routines of subsistence sharecropping rather than risk leaping into the urban unknown.

They married when Daisy was eighteen. Rail worked the fields by hand and operated various pieces of farm machinery like the tractor-mounted seeder. Mama's first child, a daughter, was born when she was nineteen. Ed was born a year later, the first of six sons born in succession, followed by another daughter. The rapidly expanding family lived in a tight wooden dwelling, perhaps 450 square feet divided into four small rooms. The home had a tin roof and a front porch shaded by a tin awning. It was set back from Gobler Road, surrounded by a sea of farmland.

Everything that mattered was nearby. The gray cinder-block Gobler School, with multiple grades crammed into a single classroom, was a five-minute walk up the road. The Baptist church, hand-built by parishioners and kept white with fresh paint as funds allowed, was down the road in the other direction, a few minutes' walk. Ten minutes further was the post office, a boxlike space with a hinged half-door that allowed the postal clerk to lean over and chat with customers checking the bank of windowed mail boxes embedded in the far wall. Adjoining the post office was the general store, owned by a white entrepreneur who also sold automobiles and farm equipment. The general store stocked dry goods, utilitarian hardware, household utensils. The Hightowers, like other families, kept a running tab. All transactions were on credit. The store's owner knew them, knew where they lived, and knew when payday at the fields came around.

Dozens of relatives — "relatives galore," as Ed described it — Millers, Burtons, and Hightowers, aunts and uncles and cousins, all of them émigrés from Mississippi, also lived along Gobler Road and the long straight nameless dirt roads branching into the boundless fields beyond. It almost seemed that the entire tract of farmland west of Deering and east of Highway NN belonged to their clan. And in some ways it did. They owned their houses. Some owned the nearby fields. Even the cemetery, a rectangular patch of weedy earth delineated from the surrounding farmland only by a scattering of rocks, would eventually resemble a family plot, so many of the graves would be Hightowers or Millers or immediate kin.

Residing in houses of nearly the same size, each made of the same basic materials, boards and beams and tin roofs, set on land as treeless and undifferentiated as anything you'd find in the Big Agra tracts of Nebraska, Gobler was a close-knit community of hardworking people who couldn't help but notice, when they finally had time to look up and contemplate a future beyond each day's pressing demands, that the country was changing and maybe for the better.

Hightower began "chopping" cotton the summer after second grade. At 5:30 a.m., he would set off in the company of his father, mother, and older sister. The sun would be rising as they waited on Gobler Road for the arrival of the flatbed truck that the field boss had arranged to cart them to each day's assigned tract. As younger brothers came of age, they joined the brigade.

The work was hot, laborious, repetitive, grueling drudgery. With bare hands, raw from blisters until thickened with callouses, or using a homemade Kaiser blade, they dug up and cut down the weeds around the cotton plant. This was "chopping" cotton. Later in the growing season, deeper into summer, the task turned to picking the cotton. Cotton bolls, tough and prized for their lint, had to be pulled by hand from the seedpod and placed in a burlap sack that was dragged along the row until it was full.

The workday was twelve hours or longer, with a fifteen-minute break every couple of hours, and a half hour for lunch. Children worked alongside the adults, moving in a long slow progression up one row and down the next. The rising sun grew insufferably hot. Field hands wore straw hats for whatever small protection they provided. "Sunstroke?" Hightower laughed at the quaint notion that the health and comfort of the field hand was ever a consideration. "We didn't know what sunstroke was."

The compensation system was straightforward, blunt. You were not paid by the hour. You were not paid by the job. You were not paid on the basis of any subjective evaluation of performance. And you were certainly not paid for superior effort or exemplary attitude. You were paid solely and explicitly on the basis of measurable results. Pay was contingent on quantity picked as measured in pounds. Burlap sacks stuffed with cotton were hauled to the edge of the field and loaded onto a truck. The truck then drove onto an industrial scale situated a few miles away in the compound that housed the ginning operation. Labor = picked cotton = aggregate weight = pay per pound. What did the income from this sweltering, backbreaking work average out to in terms of dollars per hour? For most, it was too depressing to calculate.

Two hundred twenty-five pounds per day was the quota that Ed's father and mother set for themselves. The children were given a dispensation, but not much of one, based on their age. For Ed, it was one hundred seventy-five pounds until his early teens. Then, he was expected to produce as much as a man.

I mention Hightower's cotton-field summers not simply to highlight the harsh circumstances of his upbringing. The world of sports, and other arenas of intense competition, are often populated by men and women whose fierce determination to succeed was forged of brute necessity. What's fascinating about the challenges Hightower has surmounted is that it almost requires a kind of time-travel to conjure them, so vastly different is the modern world. A skinny child beneath a blazing southern sun in a frayed straw hat, half-hidden amid a cultivated row of emerald-green plants bursting white with the precious bolls, is a scene from a prior century. Or an underdeveloped third world nation.

I asked him once, a bit thoughtlessly, if he had anything like fond memories of those bygone days. Subconsciously, I was probably channeling some romanticized antebellum hooey brought to the silver screen by MGM, or maybe a country ballad crooned by a syrup-sweet tenor lamenting the homespun virtues of the gritty bygone rural life. "No," he snapped with his crisp trademark enunciation, chuckling dismissively at the very suggestion such labor had any redeeming upside. "No, no, no, no! It was hard, hard work."

Recently I visited Gobler with Hightower. I'd never been anywhere quite like it. A remote plateau deep in central Mexico, unending and hot, might be the best comparison. I can only trust Hightower's assessment that not much had changed in fifty years. The land was still naked of trees and given over entirely to farming, mostly cotton. Houses were still few and far between. A tractor groaned in the distance. The air was thick with humidity and utterly still. Several of the houses Hightower would visit as a child, because an aunt or cousin lived there, remained almost as he'd left them, weatherworn and unpainted. The general store had closed. The post office was open, tentatively, a few hours each day.

The Gobler School, which Hightower had attended until fourth grade, survived only as a remnant, like some Mayan archaeological site. Fragments remained of the cinder-block outer walls, but the roof was completely gone. The vacant interior, where earnest public school pedagogy once flourished in buzzing classrooms, now buzzed with insects and flies, overgrown with leafy saplings and sprawling bushes.

When Hightower's education began, only blacks attended the Gobler School. School segregation was absolute and, save for the distant rumblings of social protests elsewhere, largely unquestioned. Separate but equal was a cover story that still held sway. Whites in the area attended the Deering School.

As the oldest boy, Ed was not simply expected to serve as role model for the younger siblings; it was demanded of him. His parents' marriage was already rocky and would soon end in divorce. His father, gregarious and popular, worked long days in the fields. But that hard work did not extend to the challenge of keeping eight children in line. His mother, known as Mama, a moniker that carried within the family the utmost respect, took that one on with a vengeance.

Mama's workload, chopping cotton plus managing the kids, left her with neither time nor patience for telling anyone twice what needed to be done. Her rules were ironclad and simple to understand. You did what she told you to do, you did it the way she told you to do it, and you did it when she wanted it done. Any deviation, and you got whupped.

A switch made of a supple tree branch was her tool of choice, although a belt sometimes sufficed. Employed with force on a child's rump, it sent a message that lingered both for the tearful recipient and everyone else within earshot. "My mom was a country woman," explained Ed's brother Clarence, the former president of the Urban League of Minneapolis and currently on the board of trustees of Minnesota State Colleges and Universities. With droll understatement, he added, "She did not believe in time-outs."

Around the house, Ed was Mama's second-in-command, "our in-house dad," according to Clarence. There were chickens and hogs and a vegetable garden to care for. There was cooking and baking to be done on a wood stove. Coals from the stove supplied their heat. The house lacked running water. Clothes were washed at the nearby levee. A backyard well supplied water for cleaning dishes and other household needs.

Sundays were given over entirely to church. Attired in the best clothes they could muster, dresses for Mama and the girls, slacks and clean cotton shirts for the boys and their father, the family made the short walk to the Baptist church and stayed there, praying and singing and absorbing the fervent sermons, from midmorning through the afternoon.

It got very warm inside, and there were days when Ed and his brothers would have rather been scampering on the ball field or fishing or hunting crawdaddys in the creek or doing almost anything except sitting up straight on a hard wooden pew. They sat all in a row in the same pew, the Hightower children with Mama at the end, keeping watch. One glance from her, eyes burning, jaw set, was all it took to put a quick end to any goofing off. Misbehavior was not tolerated on her watch, and she always seemed to be watching.

In second grade, Ed had a teacher who occasionally came to class drunk, or so it seemed to the children who had a fairly sharp eye for the telltale signs of adult inebriation. She was sloppy, disorganized, a cause for ridicule not respect. Ed complained to his mother. Mama's response was baffling. She reminded him that the teacher was in charge; do as you're told. Years later he would gain a more nuanced insight into the need for such inflexible dictums, as well as the downside in sticking by them. But Mama's rule was unquestioned, and it was evident to Ed how she viewed such situations: it was not the place for underlings to evaluate authority. The social order was governed by a system that bestowed benefits according to rules that it chose to call fair, whether they were or not. His time and energy would be far better spent learning to navigate those rules than questioning them. Second-guessing the system was as fruitless as wishing for a change in the weather. The Hightower children would do things "the right way." And the right way, as Mama saw it, was not a complicated concept. Work hard. Do what's expected. Give back.

This last command, "give back," was a somewhat unconventional one to press upon young children. And it was not at all clear at the time what Mama meant by it. But she never failed to hammer it home. Likewise with another dictum, stated with the force of law. "You know when you are doing somebody right," she would instruct her children, including the future referee. "And you know when you're doing somebody wrong."

In fifth grade, everything changed. Public schools in southeast Missouri finally began integrating the upper grades. The year was 1963. Instead of a short amble down Gobler Road, Ed, along with a handful of other children as excited and apprehensive as himself, boarded a dust-caked yellow bus that would transport him to the previously all-white Deering School.

Whereas segregation in southeast Missouri was not as viciously imposed as it was in Mississippi, it was nonetheless an unmistakable feature of everyday life. Hayti, where the Hightower family periodically went to shop for shoes or school clothing, had a white population that owned the stores and ran the town. Hayti Heights, on the western fringe of town, was where blacks lived. The closest the two races came to comfortably sharing the same space was in the Missouri Theater, a 350-seat movie house operated by the family that also owned the furniture store next door. It was such a thrill for the Hightower children to go to the movies — it happened rarely, "when things were good," in Ed's words — that being made to sit upstairs in the balcony and far from the screen was an indignity that was happily endured.

"Separate educational facilities are inherently unequal" was the signal conclusion of the landmark *Brown v. Board of Education* Supreme Court ruling that refuted the long-standing segregationist contention that our nation's egalitarian ideals were happily intact so long as racially divided school systems were "separate but equal." The court ruling was issued in 1954. But the seventeen states that were being explicitly ordered to reform, including Missouri, proceeded with caution. Few believed that integration would instantly blossom into full equality as the result of a Supreme Court edict. "Do what you're told," Mama instructed Ed. "Keep your mouth shut. Listen to your teachers. I don't want to hear about any problems."

In the third grade, Miss Jackson was Ed's assigned teacher. She was beautiful, he thought, and very smart. He fantasized getting married to her.

Most importantly, Miss Jackson felt *he* was smart. Whether he truly stood out as an exceptionally promising up-and-comer, the kind of raw unpolished gem that teachers instinctually scout for, is unclear. It's entirely possible that Miss Jackson was simply the kind of devoted educator who treated every child as special, the kind of teacher Superintendent Hightower would one day make a priority of recruiting for *his* school system.

Third grade with Miss Jackson was a turning point. She was the teacher who flipped the switch, who turned on the juice. With Miss Jackson, Ed began to believe that he was not simply dutiful, hardworking, determined, earnest, and trustworthy, all of which he already knew about himself. Now he believed he might be smart. Now he believed he had not simply the capacity to solve the basic three R's of schoolwork, but to excel at them.

He believed as a matter of faith that success in school would be rewarded. He believed, since his mother insisted it was true, that achievement in the classroom was the stepping-stone to larger achievements. And it was the only category of achievement, given their circumstance, remotely within reach. School was his chance. Mama said so. Miss Jackson said so. His American history textbook, in its own way, said so.

At the Deering School, select students were given the assignment of patrolling the school grounds outside the building and, before and after the school day, keeping the student drop-offs and pickups orderly. Students awarded this role were usually sixth graders who'd proven themselves worthy. It was a coveted status, replete with a distinguishing white canvas belt to be proudly strapped across the chest. The job was awarded on a rotating basis to students of exemplary academic achievement and unblemished personal comportment. Ed's A average and commendable classroom behavior clearly would allow him to qualify.

From his earliest days at Deering, Ed had his sights set on this prize. With a sharp eye for the social pecking order and a yen to be at the top of it, he could easily envision himself directing the other students when to stop and wait, and when they were free to go. Student patrols were invested with an authority that other children must heed. Their responsibilities, symbolized by the belt, reflected a maturity of judgment and dependability that set them apart from their peers. They were also all white.

His first year at Deering, there was no expectation of being named a patrol leader. By the time Ed entered sixth grade, however, he felt certain his time had arrived. Hadn't he fulfilled every requirement, the high marks in his coursework and the commendations for being a solid school citizen? But as the year unfolded, fall into winter into spring, it became evident that he was being passed over. Other students of lesser accomplishment were being designated instead. And he was pretty sure he knew the reason.

One evening after washing the dishes, he approached Mama with his frustrations. He was consistently on the honor roll. He'd not been tardy or absent. He'd never once been reprimanded by a teacher and was often praised. By every single standard that was said to govern the choice of student patrols, he'd earned it. Racism, a term he was aware of but discouraged from dwelling on or invoking, was the only possible explanation, as far as he could tell. Bitterly, he complained, "It's not . . ."

Mama scowled. She knew where this was going.

He wanted his mother to share in his hurt and outrage. "It's not fair and it's because . . ."

Her scowl hardened. Mama was well aware of this line of complaint; she'd been hearing it all her life. She knew more than her children would ever know about racial prejudice and its many insidious cruelties. She knew all about deviousness and rank hypocrisy. With private disgust, she'd witnessed countless examples of the pompous lip service white folk paid to the noble concept of equality and the pale excuse for the real thing she encountered every day.

All Ed wanted was for his mother to reassure him that, yes, she understood what had happened, that he'd been dealt with unfairly and for the ugliest of reasons. Because his skin was dark.

Sympathy is not what he received. Discrimination might be an obstacle, in Mama's thinking, but it was no excuse. "What does being a school patrol have to do with anything?" she snapped. "What does it matter? Do your work. Get good grades. Do as you're told."

. . .

In 1966, Mama, having separated from her husband, moved the family north to Alton, Illinois, across the river from St. Louis. Her older brother Mose had made this move, from Gobler, a few years previously and had easily found work. Alton at the time was an industrial boomtown with an array of thriving manufacturing operations. Owen-Illinois Glass, once the largest manufacturer of glass in the world, had a plant in Alton, as did the Alton Box Board Company and Laclede Steel, maker of wire, pipe, tubing, and reinforcing bars. All along Broadway, a busy commercial stretch overlooking the Mississippi, were signs advertising "Help Wanted." Factory work, Mose felt, was the best way for Mama to provide for her large family.

Mama was then in her mid-thirties. She had the prominent cheekbones, narrow scrutinizing eyes, and full lips that would be most closely reproduced in her eldest son. Relocating to an urban environment would severely test her capacity to micromanage eight school-age children. But the promised benefits of better work for better pay could not be ignored. Gobler with its dusty roads where you could literally see someone coming a mile away had been a wonderful comfort. Their new life would unfold in bustling Alton with its swarm of strangers.

At the time the family moved, Ed was starting his freshman year at Alton High. This was his first experience living with indoor plumbing. It was the first time he lived along a street that was paved, and walked to the bus on sidewalks. It was a world alive with stimulation and new social opportunities. Mama doubled down on the discipline. She had no choice.

She landed a job working various machines at the Olin Company's East Alton Winchester Division that specialized in making ammunition for a range of firearms. Olin's rampant expansion, from its inception in 1892 as a regional supplier of blasting powder for midwestern coal mines to its successful twentieth-century diversification into the pharmaceutical (Squibb) and chemical (Olin Mathieson) industries, would have an ironic culmination in 2004 when the Winchester Division, where Mama eventually worked for thirty-five years, relocated to Mississippi to save on labor costs.

Mama signed up for the night shift so she could be home in the morning to get the younger children off to school and, following an abbreviated sleep, be awake in the afternoon to oversee their homework and chores.

Many families have pet anecdotes they trot out to enlighten the unfamiliar listener as to who they really are and what makes them tick. For the Hightower family it is this: On only one occasion was Mama ever contacted by a school official about a behavior problem involving any of her children. One time over the course some twenty-five years. One time during a span of hundreds of academic grading periods. One time in the long, arduous, lockstep progression of eight children, six of them boys, through the problem-ridden minefield of K-12 public school education. One time. For one son. And nobody ever forgot it.

It was Robert, the fifth youngest boy. The deed that triggered the incident seems trivial in retrospect. "Smarting off," is how Ed remembers it, and he remembers it with a seasoned educator's bemused chuckle at the explosion that followed. It occurred in Mr. Bentley's class at Central Junior High, first thing in the morning. Robert was asked by the teacher to tuck in his shirttail and remove his ball cap. He refused. He was then commanded more forcefully by Mr. Bentley to tuck the shirt in and take off the cap. Again, Robert refused. A standoff developed.

Another teacher, passing in the hallway, caught wind of it and promptly informed the principal. The principal arrived at Mr. Bentley's classroom, and confirmed what was taking place. The principal returned to his office to phone Mama.

Mama was home that morning to meet an Avon sales manager. Ever industrious, she was cultivating a sideline in repping Avon beauty and personal care products. After taking the call from the junior high principal, Mama turned to her Avon visitor and excused herself, stating that there was a young man she "needed to go to school to take care of."

The principal had requested Mama to get to school within fifteen minutes to fetch her son. Mama replied, "I'll be there in five."

Robert, who was employed for twenty-six years as a transportation coordinator for a charter bus company in the Twin Cities and now works as a private security officer, remembers only that, "she got there too soon."

She arrived with a leather belt.

The principal told her she was to take Robert home. "I am not taking him home," she informed the principal. "I'm going to deal with him right here."

Robert was shocked when she marched into his classroom. She instructed him to move to the rear of the room. With twenty other students, and Mr. Bentley, watching in stunned silence, Mama proceeded to lash her son across his bottom, several times, with conviction.

"The teacher was crying," Robert recalls "My classmates were crying. And so was I."

When it was over, Mama instructed Robert to return to his desk. "You are here to learn and to listen. And to be respectful," she stated.

Then she promptly departed.

"From then on," recalls Mama, a formidable chocolate-skinned woman in her eighties, with a note of triumph, "they [that is, her children and everyone else in the community who learned of the incident] had themselves a story to tell."

The Hightower home on Adams Court looked downhill across bustling Broadway toward the Mississippi River. The household was one very tight ship, and it stayed afloat and stayed on course so long as precious time and energy were not diverted. All the children, teenagers included, had to be home by 9:00 p.m. Everybody had chores to perform and all held after school jobs in town when they were old enough. Within their first year in Alton, Mama had saved enough money to buy a small shoeshine storefront on Broadway, half a block from where they lived. Ed and all his siblings worked there at various times. Extra income was only one component of Mama's strategy in acquiring the shoeshine shop. "If they aren't working," she liked to generalize about youngsters with too much time on their hands, "they'll be stealing."

Mama retained, and periodically exercised, veto power over which friends her children were allowed to bring home and whose homes they were allowed to visit. Any child about whom Mama "had a feeling" was summarily banned, no questions asked, no explanation offered. Mama understood that this degree of oversight was heavy-handed and, in the minds of some, socially unacceptable. "People thought I thought my children were better than theirs," Mama explained. "And they were right."

She was the despot who laid down the law. In her absence, it was Ed who took over, serving at times as the enforcer. "Ed was responsible for getting us to school," according to Clarence. "And for homework, for getting us to sports practices, for cooking and washing clothes and ironing." When all that was required of Ed was to manage his siblings by means of setting the proper example, all went quite smoothly. When harsher measures were called for, he was prepared to act as Mama's proxy.

Her shift at Olin ended at 8:00 a.m. Ed oversaw the mornings. It was Mama's rule that she be notified of any alteration in anyone's routine. There were simply too many moving parts for her to countenance ad hoc improvisations. One time Clarence left the house early to get to the schoolyard to play pick-up basketball before classes began. Heading to school early to play ball was not the problem. Failing to inform Ed was.

"He whupped me that night," Clarence recalled with a bemused chuckle (that phrase, "bemused chuckle," has appeared previously and will likely be used again, for it succinctly conveys the head-shaking amazement, tinged with admiration, with which the Hightower siblings reflect on their harsh, old-school upbringing) at how such outmoded disciplinary measures strike contemporary ears, including his own. "He took off his belt and whupped me."

In his senior year, Ed experienced one of those minor yet somehow pivotal events that get lionized in the inspiring accounts of historical figures and people of noteworthy accomplishment. George Washington and the cherry tree. Steve Jobs dropping out to study calligraphy. Michael Jordan getting cut from his high school team. That sort of thing.

"Principal for the day" was an honorific that Alton High, like many schools, had instituted in order to motivate student performance and grant distinction to those who deserved it. Not every student would have coveted such an honor. No doubt it was privately mocked by some, and dismissed by others as silly or meaningless. It wasn't like being captain of the football team or landing a lead role in the school play or being named valedictorian. It was merely a designation granted periodically to a student on the basis of a range of imprecise and subjective criteria. Still, Ed wanted it. As an athlete (varsity basketball and baseball), mentor to younger students, and honor-roll regular, he felt he qualified. This time he was not overlooked.

On the appointed day, he marched upstairs to the principal's private office. He was invited to attend a faculty and staff meeting. He stood alongside the principal outside his office as he surveyed the busy hallways (Alton High had nearly 3,000 students) during the passing periods. He got to plop into the principal's swivel chair; from there, he was able to peer through a plate glass window at the busy work of school secretaries in the adjoining room; if he needed anything, who knows but they might respond to his command? He got to hunker over the desktop telephone console and, after receiving instructions, was allowed to speak, with precise diction, into the intercom.

He issued the morning announcements for all the school to hear, spelling out details of tomorrow's all-school assembly and today's after-school club meetings and athletic contests. Reading off mimeographed notes, he was careful to follow the script. This was not the occasion for personal remarks. His voice was a pleasant surprise. It emerged from his throat a notch deeper than normal, sounding more authoritative than he'd thought possible.

The opportunity did not awaken old insecurities; on the contrary, it seemed to him that he grew, almost magically, from it. He would forever remember how satisfying it was to know that unseen others, kids he knew and ones he didn't, hundreds of them, were listening.

He'd watched his mother steer the family through troubled waters, and he'd shouldered, without complaint, the responsibilities of a stand-in dad. Now, as principal for the day, he'd had a taste, a peek, a quick bright flash, verging on epiphany. This job of overseeing all the moving pieces of a complex system, collaborating with others and deciding what's best, did not feel all that strange to him or impossible. In fact, it was a job he could imagine himself performing.

ONE TOUGH BRACKET

To explore how the art of officiating basketball is taught, if it can be taught, and how challenging it may be to master, if it can be mastered, I attended a summertime instructional camp at Providence College in Rhode Island. Books, manuals, YouTube uplinks aside, the craft is most effectively passed down the way fine crafts have been since time immemorial, master to neophyte, veteran to rookie, old salt to novice.

The camp was run by Michael Stephens, a smooth, efficient, churchgoing man of forty whose rapid rise through the ranks of aspiring refs was the direct result of having been "discovered" at a summer camp. Stephens, raised in a rough neighborhood in Providence's West End and currently the city's director of recreation, achieved minor distinction during a 2009 Big East tournament contest that he was not even assigned to officiate. He was comfortably seated behind the scorer's table in his capacity as a standby ref for the Syracuse–Seton Hall game — essentially, he was an understudy who needed to be available to step in should an emergency arise — when several players squared off for what loomed as an imminent brawl. Like an off-duty firefighter tearing after a blaze on the first whiff of smoke, Stephens leapt over the table and dashed onto the floor. A photo of the incident appeared in the *New York Times*, showing Stephens at mid-court in civilian garb as he plants himself squarely in the path of an enraged Seton Hall power forward half a foot taller. The confrontation defused,

Stephens returned to the stands, and from there he uneventfully watched the remainder of the game.

Stephens' ref camp was situated in Begley Arena, a vast indoor space with the approximate shape and dimensions of an airplane hangar. There were five basketball courts with games taking place simultaneously on each. The acoustics were not the best, and the noise generated by so many games involving high-energy athletes was a bit bewildering. The squeak and chuff of rubberized soles on the synthetic surface, the shouts from coaches and players, the thump-thump-thump of the dribbled balls, and, yes, the piercing screech of the referees' whistles, made for an oddly reassuring kind of cacophony.

The games were all regional AAU-level contests. The players ranged in age from fourteen to eighteen. They were enrolled in a parallel two-day skills camp, the nearly continuous games of which would serve as test kitchens for the referee campers. The several dozen ref campers, eager to hone their skills and possibly catch the eye of one of the senior instructors, were invariably earnest, diligent, obedient, ready and willing to learn.

As the morning session began in the chilled air-conditioning of the field house, I plunked down beside Jamie Luckie, a veteran ACC and Big East ref and camp instructor. Luckie had just conducted a concise Cliff's Notes briefing for the ten campers, ranging in age from early twenties to late thirties, under his tutelage. He sat in a plastic folding chair that he'd strategically situated five yards behind the baseline corner of the court, a clipboard on his lap. Silver-haired and spry with a naturally mirthful expression that managed to fall just short of outright puckishness, he clearly gave serious thought to the mechanics of his trade.

The players whose games these fledgling refs would officiate were not exactly roundball thoroughbreds. They were not, for the most part, particularly large, or athletic, or well coached.

The quality of the play was scrappy, the stakes were nil. Nobody appeared to be watching the action except for those referees assigned to do so, the referees waiting their turn to get onto the court, and instructors like Luckie who were there to observe, teach, and evaluate.

I was skeptical that very much could be discerned about a young ref's true potential in conditions that were so understated and free of stress. Instead of the cold dagger stare of Bo Ryan or Rick Pitino, you had a frazzled assistant gym teacher from Portland, Maine, who was primarily concerned with allotting equal playing time to each of his registration-fee-paying athletes. Instead of the insanity-inducing cacophony of shrieking partisans crammed into a sold-out arena, there were only the timeless gymnasium sounds of thumping balls and squeaking sneakers. It all seemed a very pale proxy for the nerve-racking pressure of the real thing. These refs, for the most part, appeared to be at least as athletic and generally larger than the teenage players. That toughest of all calls, goaltending, was not likely to appear on this syllabus.

Still, Luckie was a model of pedagogic diligence. Raised in a sports-oriented family in rural Ogdensburg, New York, where his father was director of the Boys and Girls Club, he, like other elite refs, took a craftsman's pride in his work, even if nobody outside the profession cared to know about it. Listening to him break down the complex practice of officiating into ever more granular components, striving to convey this knowledge through a combination of punchy aphorisms ("the closer you look, the less you see"), hands-on manipulation (placing one camper here, another there, by way of explaining secondary-defender infractions), and personal demonstration (showing the optimal way to rapidly shuffle sideways up-court while keeping eyes steadily trained on the action), he reminded me of an old-world Hungarian violin maestro schooling a class of impetuous prodigies.

As with learning to play a musical instrument, the rudiments of officiating can be acquired through close study of instructional manuals — Referee Enterprises out of Franksville, Wisconsin, publishes some excellent material — or by perusing a wide selection of YouTube selections that demo everything from proper hand signals to the fine points of protecting the shooter from deviousness on the part of the defender. Back in the day, pre-Internet, a number of VHS (video home system for you trivia buffs) tutorials, smartly scripted with high production values, were developed to demonstrate sports officiating. One featured a young up-and-comer in the profession, Ed Hightower.

Hightower gazed into the camera from a barstool perch. He was dressed in a dark gray shirt that fit snugly on his athletic frame. Speaking in crisp, commanding cadences (I wondered which fostered his style of verbal enunciation, his school principal's need to get the kids to listen up good or his referee's), he spelled out, utilizing classic Department of Education format, the Four Basic Elements of Officiating. Each point was illustrated with a video snippet. These video segments, with voice-over by the young Thom Brenneman, now a prominent sportscaster, depicted calls Hightower had made in real game situations. Many of them involved Jalen Rose and Chris Webber, stars from the most heralded team of that era, the University of Michigan's Fab Five (Hightower worked the fabled 1993 NCAA championship game, won by North Carolina, in which Webber, in the final seconds, incurred a technical foul by desperately signaling for a time-out when Michigan had already used all its allotment.)

"It's all about trust," Hightower stated coolly at one point in the video, as the camera cut to footage of Webber shamelessly bulldozing his way into the paint (you make the call: charge or a block?) "If I miss a rule or a play, I'll go back to the player or the coach and say, 'I missed it.' They realize you're human and can err. That builds trust."

Later in the video, Hightower added a sobering footnote for any wannabe ref hoping to improve his skills, "You're only as good as your last call."

In exploring the challenges of basketball refereeing, I'd grown fond of contemplating its possible metaphorical relevance to other facets of our individualistic, competitive, free-market society. Professing to value fairness while awarding first prize to the contestant who succeeds by elbowing their opponent aside struck me as a contradiction not limited to the sports world, and one worth pondering. The referees I met, including Hightower, showed scant enthusiasm for such contemplations.

Still, I remained convinced that the refs, despite their refusal to come right out and say so, were people possessed of a special insight. Many of them employed pithy phrases eloquently summarizing insights born of their experience, and these seemed at least as ripe for general audience consumption as what you get in the unabashedly prescriptive self-help titles authored by elite coaches. *Bounce Back: Overcoming Setbacks in Business and in Life*, by Kentucky coach John Calipari, *Leading with the Heart: Successful Strategies for Basketball, Business, and Life* by Mike Krzyzewski, and Rick Pitino's *Success Is a Choice: Ten Steps to Overachieving in Business and Life* may be just what a fellow needs to get his sorry ass to the next level. But I wouldn't know; I haven't read them.

A couple of Hightower's stock referee phrases were ones he employed just as vehemently around the school department. "It's not about who's right; it's about what's right." "See what you call, call what you see." "There's a difference between confidence and arrogance."

J. D. Collins, a veteran ref and supervisor of officials, once summarized his on-court responsibilities with a poetic eloquence that struck me as worthy of a mission statement, and a visionary one at that. "Our job," Collins said, "is to absorb the chaos, create calm, and provide hope that the outcome will be fair."

Amen.

I perched on a folding chair beside Luckie as he directed a new crew of campers to take the court and give it their best with a hapless U-16 game between Nashua, New Hampshire, and Framingham, Massachusetts. As Luckie expounded on the skills these novices would need to succeed, I felt like Carlos Castaneda by the campfire with the cryptic old sage Don Juan. What exactly was a college basketball referee's arcane way of knowledge, and could it benefit men and women from all walks of life? For the moment, I was prone to think it could.

Among the observations and admonitions Luckie doled out to the young refs:

"If you think you're thinking you should go there, go there!"

"That call you just made was a good one. But I don't *believe* it!"

"Young refs always ask, 'how much should I let go?' I say, 'Is it legal or illegal, and what harm did it cause?'"

"You need to have a patient whistle."

"You need to be mindful of whistle consequence."

"Plenty of guys can blow the whistle but can't manage the game. It's like being great on the driving range but not on the course."

"You need to have ownership of the play. If you're standing over there, you have no ownership."

"I tell them [the ref campers], 'Nobody's going to like you anyways. So you might as well be right.'"

So what exactly are those qualities and characteristics necessary to becoming a first-rate basketball referee?

"Communication" is always cited by refs at or near the top of the list. On first hearing this, I figured it to be an obligatory party line, like the warning always issued to grade-schoolers that neat handwriting *really* does matter, in homework and in life. Sure, communication matters. But why make such a big deal out of it?

"We're like actors," Hightower explained. "We need to make our audience *believe* we are right."

This means letting an irate coach know why a call went against his team, giving him an opportunity to be heard, and knowing when, and how, to let the coach know that the case is closed and it's time to move on. "You have to allow a coach to have his say," said Hightower. "Up to a point."

Communicating *with each other*, as teammates, is as important for refs as it is for players. It's chaotic out there. Individually, refs on the court often lack the full, 360-degree context that surrounds a call they must make. A ref whistling a traveling violation may not have seen the push from behind that caused it, but his fellow ref may have.

Officiating involves "optics." Each call, each decree, *each non-call*, must be dressed up in the very finest attire. Crisp hand signals, sharp whistles, no vacillation, no hint of bafflement or indecision. In response to my observation that there must be some occasions when a ref might want to pause just a moment or two to ponder what he's seen before rendering a verdict, Hightower emphatically disagreed. "You are there in order to render that final decision. The quicker you make a decision, the better off for everybody."

These calls do not, contrary to what one might conclude from the histrionics of some of the participants, carry life-or-death consequences. They are not Oval Office decisions to send in troops.

"Why," lamented Hank Nichols, the former head of NCAA officials and a man fully aware of the heresy he was espousing, "can't the coach just say, 'Yeah, we got a bad call and we lost the game' without making such a big stink out of it? You know, that bad call we got is part of basketball too."

Bad calls are part of basketball too? Now there's a novel insight!

Nichol's point, familiar to every referee but generally left unsaid for the obvious reason that it could be easily mischaracterized as an excuse, was that a referee's blown call is no different in its unintended, unplanned, unpredictable impact than, say, a badly overthrown pass that caroms off a fingertip straight through the hoop. Sports are one of America's great object lessons in the fortuitous benefits of dumb luck. "You're going to make mistakes," Hightower said. "You only hope the 2 percent of the time you're wrong doesn't effect the game."

A ref's physical appearance supplements his authority. Image might not be "everything," but it counts for something. Whereas there's no single, prescribed, straight-from-central-casting look for officials, some broad parameters exist, outside of which it becomes difficult to be effective. Even if a guy can sprint the floor like Usain Bolt. Even if he's as sharp with the law as Judge Judy. "The perception battle," is how refs put it, referring to that blend of factors, appearance included, that help a ref assert his authority.

We Americans have our preferred cultural images, and the preferred image for authority hovers somewhere between the square-jawed state trooper with mirrored sunglasses and the bifocaled elder in black robes peering down from the bench.

Luckie told of pulling an otherwise capable camper aside to snap an iPhone picture. Luckie then held the image to the camper's face so he could see exactly which of his physical features the players and coaches would invariably focus on: slight pot belly accentuated by distended zebra stripes, head tilted with a hint of fatigue, shirt untucked at the right hip. 'Nuff said.

"A sense of the game" is another quality often cited. Refs need to be aware of what each team is attempting to do on offense and defense, and it helps to know particulars about each squad and the priorities of each coach. Refs need to see all ten players yet simultaneously zero in on their primary area of concentration. They need to be aware of glaring size inequalities, especially in the post (the player with a decided height disadvantage is probably going to compensate by pushing harder than is legal or try to fool the ref into thinking he got pushed by the bigger guy), and be vigilant for the ways that other player disparities, foot speed, for example, will affect play. Refs need be able to intuit incipient shifts in momentum and be alert to the possibility that coaches too, especially when the action gets frantic, may play a role.

"Say a team scores five straight baskets," Hightower explained. "I'm going to be looking over at the coach: is he going to call time-out? Or a player is putting the ball in from out-of-bounds and he's under pressure. I'm counting, one, two, three . . . I'm looking around. Something's going to happen. Four. I'm thinking, come on, coach. Come on, player."

"Game management" is another vital capability. "Calling the game is only 25 percent," according to Karl Hess, an esteemed veteran ref who achieved additional, unwanted renown in 2012 for summoning the Raleigh police to evict two former legendary North Carolina State players, Tom Gugliotta and Chris Corchiani, from the stands for heckling him during a game. "Fifty percent is managing people. Twenty-five percent," he concluded, "is luck."

Foremost among the game management chores is keeping the hotheads in line. "We all start the game as adults," said Tom O'Connor, a veteran ref who never made it to the elite level but nonetheless saw his fair share of misbehavior. "By the end of the game some coaches and some players deteriorate to childhood. It's our job to pick them back up." Hess, who holds a PhD in marriage and family counseling, added, "If athletics aren't handled right, it becomes a bastion of narcissism."

Making certain the game clock, shot clock, and scoreboard are functioning are ultimately the referee's responsibility. Likewise, getting discarded paper cups swept away before action resumes after a time-out or removing potential hazards, such as photographers encroaching on the baseline or obstreperous fans inching too close for comfort. The fastidious ref oversees the court like a neat-freak homeowner hosting a dinner party; any blemish, no matters who's fault, is a sign of personal failing.

"Game management" is also a term of art, with its explicit implication that the contest is, ultimately, a performance to be appreciated by spectators. In this sense, game management means something parallel to what "let's go out there and give 'em a great show" means to an orchestra conductor or theater director.

"Flow" is the name for this aesthetic value. "Good refs let the flow happen," said Rick Pitino in our discussion of referee attributes. Pitino cited as a memorable example the 1992 NCAA East Regional finals — the Christian Laettner overtime buzzer beater — when his Kentucky team was on the losing end, 104–103 in overtime, of a game officiated in just that way. (While acknowledging that refs "have one of the most difficult jobs in America for the compensation they make," Pitino has never been reluctant to criticize. "The referees' biggest problem is that these are some of the greatest athletes in the country, eighteen- to nineteen-year olds, and the refs have to be in great condition to chase these kids around. Some of them can't keep up, and they should call it quits."

Let it flow. It brings refs no joy to have to call foul after foul. They understand perfectly well that fans grow impatient when breakneck action is continuously interrupted by a boring parade of whistle tweets and foot-dragging players lining up for free throws. Skilled refs send early signals as to what's permissible and what's not. "If you can talk them out of silly fouls in the first half," said Irv Brown, a former ref and current Denver radio talk show personality, "you're going to have a great game." Brown would try to convey this point not only with his whistle but with words. "I'd say to the guys in the post, 'don't lean on each other and I'll let you play.'" Likewise, Hightower preferred to warn players away from needless infractions with a little preventive policing. "I might say, 'Hey, number 51, you're spending too much time in the lane. You've got to get out of there or I'm going to call it.'"

While it is the ref's hope that a few early, strategic whistles will do the trick and the offending types of maneuvers will be appropriately halted, there is only so much he can do to influence unruly teams desperate to win. The style of play is ultimately not theirs to determine. As Art Hyland, head of Big East officials has pointed out, "What happens if you have a team who loves to foul and they don't think you're going to call it? It's a disadvantage to one team if you're allowed to hand check. But it's not a disadvantage when you only call two or three a game when they're actually fouling twelve or fifteen times a game."

Rich Falk, before becoming Big Ten supervisor of officials, coached perpetual underdog Northwestern. His squads, frequently outclassed in terms of foot speed and offensive firepower, adopted a strategy of milking the shot clock and playing with more physical contact. "'Keep it flowing' is what everyone says they want," Falk said. "But I had slower teams and that wasn't to our advantage.

I coached them to make as much contact as they could get away with."

The fluidity of play is what fans most enjoy watching, and higher scoring is generally the expression of such a game. Fans like action and they like points. Big East supervisor of officials Hyland, in his preseason briefing of refs, pointed out that the prior season had seen an average decline in scoring of 1.1 points per game. Hardly a monumental number. But, like a minor decimal downtick on the Dow, an indicator to heed. League administrators, like skittish investors, are ever attuned to erosion in value.

In order to increase scoring, and with it, presumably, customer satisfaction, referees, beginning with the 2013–14 season, were instructed to more tightly enforce rules against hand checking and other defensive tactics used to impede an offensive player's movements. There was little mystery why the game had evolved in this direction. From a coaching standpoint, tough "D" was a more reliable weapon than the erratic, streaky nature of offensive play. Aggressive defense was within a coach's power to implement in a way that offense, with its vexing reliance on unpredictability, was not. But tough "D" can make for an ugly spectacle.

Predictably, the early games of the 2013–14 season saw too many fouls being whistled and too much unwanted dead time as players lined up for free throws. This predicament of being tasked to call more fouls in order to facilitate more scoring and thereby incurring, at least in the near term, even greater spectator disgruntlement, became a near-perfect microcosm of the referees' scapegoat status.

For Hightower, it was all a piece of a long-developing trend. Earlier in his career, when the sport was less a box-office extravaganza and the stakes were lower if only because the material rewards were substantially less, he'd felt entrusted, even empowered, to editorialize when the situation called for it. Pulling players aside and addressing them directly about rough play before slapping them with a foul became almost a trademark gesture for him. Fans hated it. Coaches for the most part understood. There was the letter of the law, and then there was the goal of staging the best game possible. The two were sometimes in conflict, and only the ref was in a position to negotiate an optimal solution. "When I came up, it was all about managing the game," he commented with a hint of wistfulness for a bygone era. "These days, it's more, 'just call the foul.'"

Referees, it should be noted, view themselves as fully vested partners, along with the players and coaches, in the quest to stage a fair, competitive contest that honors the core aesthetics of the sport, including flow. Ironically, they alone among the principal parties appear capable of keeping this goal in mind.

Hank Nichols, with something close to a lover's affection, remembers the best game he ever officiated. It was the 1974 ACC championship game but it might just as well have been the NCAA finals. Maryland and North Carolina State were considered the top two teams in the country, although the structure of the NCAA tournament at the time, with only a sixteen-team field, meant that only the league champion moved on to a bracket. Maryland had six players who would be drafted by the NBA and three (Len Elmore, Tom McMillen, and John Lucas) who would become pro stars. NC State was led by all-American David Thompson and 7' 4" center Tom Burleson. The game was played at breakneck speed throughout. NC State, which went on to win the NCAA championship, prevailed in overtime, 103–100. During regulation time, neither team committed a turnover. The losing team shot 62 percent for the game. Only thirty-three fouls were called, a small amount for such an intense contest that lasted an extra five minutes. According to author John Feinstein, writing in the *Washington Post*, "The 1974 [ACC] final, the last one played in which only the tournament winner could advance to the NCAA tournament, is generally considered the best game played in the event's 51-year history and perhaps one of the greatest college basketball games ever played."

Nichols, a self-effacing yet imposing presence, even in retirement, who sported a flannel lumberjack shirt for our meeting in his suburban Philadelphia living room, explained his approach in that classic contest, "We just got out of the way and let them play."

The qualities necessary to become a successful ref (see above) were always cited to me with a perplexing caveat. Namely, it was quite possible for an aspiring referee to possess all these capabilities, to know the rule book cold and have a shrewd eye for the nuances of the sport and to appear as self-assured and commanding as General Patton on the battlefield, to in effect ace every one of these tests, yet still fail to make the grade because . . . because . . . he lacked an indefinable yet somehow unmistakable X factor.

The "get it" factor was another name I heard for this nebulous, albeit vital, characteristic.

On the sideline at the Providence ref camp, I asked Luckie how he can discern — indeed, I'd asked if it *actually can be discerned* — which of the young refs might possess the requisite talent to eventually get assigned a pressure-packed showdown between, say, Syracuse and Georgetown. To answer me, he employed a rather strange analogy to, of all things, Olympic figure skating. "You can be every bit as good as the other competitors," he reasoned, "but until you've become someone known to the judges, you can't get a high score. No matter how well you perform."

Yes, that is certainly the reputation that's dogged Olympic figure skating. For decades it was perceived as a swamp of private aesthetic preferences and quasi-political prejudices made palatable through allegedly numerical forms of scorekeeping. I did not take

Luckie's comments to be an indictment of that magnitude. Rather, he was pointing out that a harsher standard gets applied to those, like these ref campers, who are novices. They will not get the benefit of doubt; indeed, there will always be doubt until such time as they have demonstrated the ability to do the job consistently. Until then, the X factor will prove elusive.

Nearly every ref I interviewed referred to this mysterious feature in one way or another. I found this particularly frustrating coming from Hightower, the educator. For if there's any axiom fundamental to education, it's that knowledge and competence are teachable and therefore acquirable. If a student, a young Ed Hightower for example, burns with a relentless drive to achieve, the theory, the belief, the assumption, the hope is that he or she *will achieve*.

Clearly, the elementary skills of competent officiating — positioning, mastery of the rulebook, communication, and so on — can be learned through diligent study and practice. Yet I was being told that the elite refs, not unlike the elite athletes they police, possess an extra-value category.

"Okay," I'd reply, pushing back. "That's interesting, this so-called get-it factor. Tell me more."

But they never could. Or would. It was a classic catch-22 exercise, trying to nudge these referees to articulate a crucial quality that they insisted was so deeply instinctual and so irreducibly the by-product of vast amounts of wildly varied crunch-time experiences as to be essentially outside the capacity of human language to describe. *You just have it*, they would say, as if that said anything at all. *It clicks. You have it. You get it.*

I briefly wondered if it was something like a secret Masonic handshake they were bound by oath not to share with the uninitiated. But I don't think so.

I think refs would gladly pin it down if they could. They're not egomaniacs striving to cultivate an aura of specialness and inscrutability. On the other hand, they know what a minor miracle it can be to successfully negotiate each game's hornet's nest of provocations. And they know not everyone can do it.

Confusion over how a person's extraordinary skill is developed runs deep. The heated debate over writer Malcolm Gladwell's "10,000 hour rule," as put forth in his popular book *Outliers: The Story of Success*, indicates that it is not just referees who get tongue-tied trying to pinpoint the fundaments of their expertise. Proficiency in activities from musicianship to athletics, Gladwell contends, can be achieved only through vast amount of practice (10,000 hours was the ballpark figure he cited, applying it to the triumphs of Bill Gates and the Beatles, among others.)

Critics, most prominently David Epstein in his book *The Sports Gene*, argued that natural talent (Usain Bolt, Michael Jordan) was the indispensable ingredient to success in sports and, by implication, other fields as well. "We've tested over ten thousand boys," Epstein quotes one South African researcher as saying, "and I've never seen a boy who was slow become fast."

The fact that academic researchers and scholars remain divided on these essential questions — Can talent be taught? Are winners made or born? — suggests that the confounding X factor offered by referees to explain how they've acquired their skill set may merely be a stand-in for the age-old nature versus nurture conundrum. Refs are not the only ones a bit mystified as to how master practitioners are able to do what they do.

The closest that Hightower, on being pressed, came to a finer distinction was to cite the way that preparedness undergirds the X factor. To illustrate, he discussed a recent "call" he'd made on behalf of the Edwardsville schools. The winter of 2013–14 had brutalized the academic calendar, with ten snow-day cancellations having already been suffered (or enjoyed, depending on perspective) by the second week in February. Making up for lost classroom time is a nightmare for school administrators, and the school calendar complications worsened as the winter continued.

The weather forecast for the greater St. Louis region, beginning on the night of February 5 and continuing through the morning hours of Wednesday, February 6, was for sleet and snow accumulations of several inches or more. Hightower prided himself on nothing so much as preparedness. His methodology with regard to looming snow cancellations was always the same. He awakened 3:00 a.m. and dispatched a handful of school buses to start running the rural northern areas of the district and report back to him with an assessment of road conditions. At 4:00 a.m., he called the police for their report on the conditions of the main arteries in town as well as rural subdivisions. At 4:30 a.m. he received a report from his director of buildings and grounds, whose crews had been out working on the sidewalks and parking lots at each of his fourteen buildings. All the while, Hightower had been studying updated weather reports via the Internet and TV.

At a little after 4:30 a.m., he determined it would be okay to proceed with a normal school day, without even needing delays in the start times. Most of the districts surrounding Edwardsville, erring on the side of safety, had made the decision the night before to cancel classes for the entire day.

"I've minimized the opportunities to make a mistake," is the way Hightower characterized this process. "When I go into a basketball game, same thing. I know the rule book. I've met before the game with my two other refs. We've discussed the two coaches and their styles of play. I'm in good shape, physically. When I go out there, it's just a matter of, do I have the intestinal fortitude to put the air in the whistle when I have to?"

. . .

The developmental stages of a referee's career, at least for those like Hightower who aspired to the elite ranks, roughly recapitulate that of the players: local youth leagues on to high school and regional AAU, then up to D-3 and junior colleges, then to mid-major "satellite" conferences, and beyond. Of the estimated more than 100,000 basketball referees working in the United States at every level, from rec leagues on up, fewer than 200 have active schedules (thirty games or more per season) working elite college games, with another 65 working in the NBA. As with players, a system for scouting out promising referees exists that is highly informal at the lower levels and grows increasingly systematized, and competitive, nearer the top. The difference between making it and *almost making it* can seem alarmingly subjective, even mercurial.

At one preseason game I met a young ref who was assigned to work with Hightower. It was one of those early-in-the-schedule arrangements between a powerhouse Big Ten team and an inexperienced, second-tier state university avid to upgrade its program's image by playing, and possibly being crushed by, a nationally ranked team. For this young ref, the game amounted to a tryout. He'd already had a few.

This was his fourth year pursuing the dream of becoming a major conference official. In his first season he'd worked three games, all preseason, involving satellite-conference teams. The second year, only two games. The third year, five. Each summer he'd diligently attended multiple camps like the one in Providence, with registration fees as high as $600 plus travel and hotel expenses. Back home, he had a thriving business as a building contractor. He had a wife and young daughter. Life was good. But college basketball officiating was what he aspired to.

Why? There was no single reason. Getting paid to stay in shape and work in a sports environment was attractive. The travel held some appeal. Whereas slogging through sleet on the Pennsylvania Turnpike can be brutal, he also understood there were holiday tournaments in places like Maui and the Bahamas where he might kick back at the turquoise pool between assignments and consider himself fortunate indeed for getting paid to be there. Most importantly, he loved the game of basketball and loved the array of physical, emotional, psychological, and strategic challenges that refereeing posed.

He'd begun by working grade school and high school games. Frustrated at not getting D-1 assignments, he'd veered into working D-3 and women's college games ("last night we had thirty people in the stands," he told me of a game he'd worked in West Virginia) until being warned that doing so might jeopardize a promotion in the men's ranks.

In short, he was doing all that he could.

An articulate African American, immensely personable and a solid citizen, he'd studied films of the games he'd worked to scrutinize his own performance, and studied video of games worked by elite refs like Hightower for cues to their success. At each ref camp he attended he made a point of seeking out the veteran instructors to ask what parts of "his game" they felt he needed to work on (one chided him for appearing too casual during time-outs, standing with hands on hips). He freely admitted he was not yet ready to handle a high-pressure assignment like a Big Ten rivalry clash or an early-round NCAA tournament game. He did, however, feel that on the basis of the excellent evaluations he'd received during the camps and the progress he'd demonstrated in the few major conference games he'd been allowed to officiate, he was nearing his goal.

To me, he seemed primed to advance. I mentioned this to Hightower and to my surprise he disagreed.

"Because there's simply no openings?" I asked.

No, that wasn't it.

"Because the process is political? He doesn't have the right connections, the right pedigree?"

That wasn't it either. "He's doing all he can do," Hightower allowed. "But he's probably reached his maximum level of competence."

I ticked off the fellow's assets. The guy looked great in zebra stripes. He was athletic and could run. He loved the sport and knew the rules cold. He was upstanding, outwardly self-assured, and would clearly be a credit to the profession. Could it be that he lacked the X factor?

"You got it."

"And there's nothing further he can do?"

Hightower gave a rueful chuckle. Probably it wasn't fair, life's arbitrary allotment of this intrinsic asset. But in his opinion not a darn thing could be done about it.

The egalitarian in me objected, and I would have thought that the concerned and supportive educator in Hightower would hold a similar attitude. "Can't you," I pressed, "spell out what it is he's missing?"

Hightower shook his head. In the broader design in which innate abilities were unevenly apportioned, some things would never be fair.

While some ambitious young refs get their shot at the big leagues, others who remain firmly convinced they've got the right stuff nonetheless languish season after season in the minors. I once read an amusing book on baseball trivia called *The Answer Is Baseball* that posed the question, "Who holds the career record for most home runs in the minor leagues?" The author, Luke Salisbury, went on to explain why this question was so intriguing. The answer involved an interesting catch-22: the slugger had to have been a player who was talented enough to have slammed numerous home runs. Yet for whatever reasons — deficient with the glove, bad on-base percentage, prone to strikeouts — he'd been consigned to the minors for the lion's share of his career.

There will always be talented men who fall short. It can happen not just to athletes but to refs.

Hightower himself had been a somewhat promising high school athlete. How promising? Well, that's always the relevant question, and the passage of time tends to provide the answer. At Alton High, he played varsity baseball and basketball, but his talent was strongest in basketball. He was quick and shrewd. He had a nice touch from outside with a smooth release that in his mind's eye he liked to think emulated that of high-scoring "Sweet Lou" Hudson of the NBA's St. Louis (later Atlanta) Hawks.

He chose to stay nearby for college and play for Southern Illinois–

Edwardsville. His first eligible season, under coach Harry Gallatin, a legendary figure who'd played for the New York Knicks (he once led the NBA in rebounding), Hightower saw a lot of playing time. The team went 7–16, after which Gallatin was replaced by a new coach with a mandate to win more games. The new coach promptly recruited six junior college players and Hightower was informed that if he wanted to keep playing college basketball he should consider transferring.

He was angry. He felt he deserved better treatment. Bitter memories of old injustices flared anew. This time, however, he dealt with the disappointment as Mama would have him do. He increased his academic course load, with the aim of graduating early. And he began refereeing intramural games, as many as he could, at $1.25 per game.

After receiving his BA in education, he was hired directly out of college to teach phys ed at one of Alton's junior high schools. He also coached cross-country, basketball, and baseball. A new agenda, one he'd previously never considered, began to take shape in his mind. Coaching came naturally and he believed he had some aptitude, particularly with basketball. He understood the strategies and fundamentals of the sport. He knew the mechanics of running a practice and had a feel for the psychodynamics of coaxing optimal performance from moody, erratic young athletes. They needed discipline and at the same time they craved encouragement. It was a delicate blend. The junior high squad he coached that first season excelled, soundly beating other local teams. The next year, a position opened up to coach the sophomore basketball team at Alton High, his alma mater. This job could be his first step up the ladder, and he already had a glimmer of where that ladder might lead. But the Alton High position was given instead to another junior high coach, one Hightower felt to be less qualified. His anger flared again.

By the age of twenty-four, he was done with playing. And done with coaching. But not done with basketball.

John Overby, the former Missouri Valley Conference supervisor of basketball officials, remembers receiving a phone call from Herm Rohrig, the Big Ten's supervisor of officials. "Johnny, I've got a good one," Rohrig reported. "He's from Alton, Illinois, and I could use your help."

Hightower had already made the leap from working intramural games at SIU–Edwardsville, sometimes five in an afternoon, to the marginally better compensated yet unquestionably more competitive interscholastic clashes between basketball-crazed towns on the Illinois side of the river. While determined to make education his primary career, Hightower wrestled with a dilemma common to referees: should he invest the time and energy, and stress and expense, needed to take his "game" to the "next level"?

The answer might seem like an obvious slam dunk: why wouldn't a guy take a shot at an opportunity to travel the countryside and appear on national TV and get paid handsomely, all for participating in some of the most exciting sporting events in the land?

But that was not quite the picture Hightower saw. In the early 1980s, compensation for reffing Division 1 contests was often a modest $150 per game plus expenses. The traveling would most likely be to midwestern college towns, fine places all, but hardly exotic. National telecasts, even if such ego gratification mattered to him, were too few and far between to be a consideration.

If Hightower chose to go for it, his primary motivation would have to be an old-fashioned one: because he craved the challenge, and because he wanted, in fact *needed*, to discover how good a referee he could become. And that ultimate test of his ability could only be confronted at the very top tier of competition.

Many referees have approached their careers with a similar

motivation. Many are ex-athletes who once dreamed of athletic glory, and often did enjoy some high school success, and perhaps a bit beyond that. But gradually they came to recognize that for all their passion for the sport, whatever sport, the cold truth was that they had already peaked and no amount of practice was going to alter that circumstance. Whatever churning inner compulsion they still harbored to face up to a challenge and triumph would have to find another outlet — if they did not choose to abandon it altogether, as so many of us do.

Hightower and his wife discussed the pros and cons. Barbara, one of eighteen children raised in Alton, grew up in circumstances every bit as difficult as those of her husband. Her father had been steadily employed at Duncan Foundry and Machine Works, maker of mining equipment and parts, but by any standard that was a lot of mouths to feed, and money was tight. While Hightower and Barbara each held demanding jobs — he was then the assistant principal of North Junior High and she was a retail clerk at Venture Department Store — their prospects for financial stability were far from guaranteed. They had no safety net.

In the summer of 1981, an instructional camp for prospective college refs was being held at Michigan State in East Lansing. Hightower understood it would be an excellent opportunity to learn firsthand from seasoned major conference officials, and he would get a chance to showcase his skills for the conference supervisors in attendance. He was convinced that, if given the opportunity, he could demonstrate that he had what it took. There was, however, quite literally, a cost.

Hightower vividly remembers the numbers the way Warren Buffet is said to recall the share price of his first purchases, when still a Columbia University business student, of Geico. The tab for enrolling in the clinic was $375. A round-trip plane ticket, St. Louis to Lansing, was $325 (room and meals were part of the package).

Seven hundred dollars was a big chunk of their savings. What exactly would be gained? That was a hard question to answer beyond pure guesswork.

On the other hand, what would it cost him if he backed away from giving it his best shot? The answer to that came more easily.

With Barbara's blessing, he decided to attend.

At home, he practiced his moves with the earnestness of a young dancer approaching a chorus-line audition. Situating himself directly in front of the full-length mirror in the bedroom of their modest home on Central Avenue, he rehearsed the mechanics. He twirled hand over hand to indicate traveling. He clutched his forearm to indicate holding. He thrust his hand with forefinger extended to signal the basket should be counted. For an intentional foul, he crossed his fists to form an X above his head. When he didn't like what he saw, he'd scowl at the mirror and repeat the performance until it looked, at least to this discerning audience of one, seamless and articulate. The first time Barbara walked in on him unsuspectingly, she shrieked in horror, *"Ed, what are you doing?"*

As vividly as Hightower recalls his cash outlay to attend the East Lansing camp, and for the same reason (it marked a landmark turning point), he recalls the conversation he had with Herm Rohrig at the end of the two-day camp. A muscular man of modest size, Rohrig carried the added stature of athletic pedigree. He'd briefly played halfback for the World War II–era Green Bay Packers after starring for the University of Nebraska. He also served as a Big Ten football referee.

Hightower felt that he'd fit in well at the camp (referees do not explicitly constitute a fraternity, but getting along with others is crucial to the teamwork of successful officiating) and had been socially accepted by his largely white peers. He'd taken pains to appear professional, in pressed slacks and ironed shirts, at meals and in the classroom. Just by looking around he could tell that this distinguished him from some of his sloppily dressed competitors.

Still, he had no idea what the supervisors thought of his abilities or what his prospects for advancement might be. This wasn't the two-hundred-meter dash. He could not glance to the sides to determine his place in the pack.

"Where do you live?" Rohrig asked him. It was the last day of camp. The question struck Hightower as somewhat trivial, but any acknowledgment from the head of Big Ten officials, even one as benign as this, counted as a positive.

"The St. Louis region," Hightower answered enthusiastically.

Rohrig sighed. "Not in St. Louis, I hope. That would disqualify you."

Disqualified? Before even being informed that he might be qualified? Hightower was perplexed. Then he remembered: the Big Ten required its officials to reside in a Big Ten state. (At the time, these were Iowa, Illinois, Wisconsin, Indiana, Ohio, and Michigan.)

Hightower could not suppress a smile. "I live in Alton, Illinois. Across the river from St. Louis."

"Well then. Drop me a note in the next couple of weeks."

Not exactly the resounding endorsement Hightower had hoped for. In fact, it smacked of being the kind of pro forma brush-off Hightower assumed most campers received out of gratitude for the hefty tuition they'd paid. Nonetheless, he followed up as requested.

There are occasions in life when the right words succinctly expressed at the right moment can make all the difference. Hightower took great pains to craft his letter. Two paragraphs long, he can recite it still by heart. The letter read:

Dear Mr. Rohrig,

Just a follow-up to the Big Ten Camp recently held at Michigan State. It was wonderful meeting you, Jim "Boomer" Bain, and George Solomon. One of my life goals is to be a Big Ten Official. You asked me to drop you a line upon returning home. It would be a dream come true if you would someday consider me for the Big Ten staff. I want to stress I do not live in the State of Missouri, but in Illinois.

I am a junior high assistant principal and I am currently working on my specialist degree to someday become a Principal and eventually a Superintendent of Schools.

Again, I know that you are busy, so thank you for such a wonderful experience at the Big Ten Camp.

Respectfully, Ed Hightower

Toward the end of summer, he received a letter on Big Ten letterhead. He opened it with the nervous apprehension familiar to college admission applicants:

"This is to inform you that beginning this season you will be added to the Big Ten satellite staff. We will contact you soon with your assignments." At that time, the Big Ten oversaw the officiating assignments at Division 2 schools such as Eastern Illinois University, Western Illinois University, Northern Iowa, and some of the independent institutions.

Yes! He'd made it.

. . .

The pool of men qualified to perform the core functions of basketball officiating, men who knew the rules and were attuned to the nuances of the sport, was fairly sizable. Those who could perform the job superbly, under pressure, night after night, were a distinctly smaller group. And a smaller subgroup still, and sorely in demand, was young African American referees.

Hightower's ref career was fortuitously timed with a push to increase the number of African American officials. The Missouri Valley had been one of the first major conferences to field teams largely made up of black players (Cincinnati's Oscar Robertson being the most heralded). In addition, the conference had recently hired two prominent black head coaches, Nolan Richardson at Tulsa and Willis Reed at Creighton.

Racial disparities in sports can be jarring, and this was particularly true in college basketball. Colleges and universities touting the success of sports teams led by young black athletes who were paid nothing beyond the cost of their schooling, and were coached by high-salaried white men with multiyear contracts underwritten by wealthy alumni and trustees who themselves were largely if not exclusively white smacked just a little too much of the old south plantation system. If that awkwardness was compounded by assigning the law-enforcement function of the game to three white dudes, as often happened, an optics problem could emerge, and that needed to be fixed.

Unpaid African Americans slugging it out for the amusement of a comfortably seated white audience was an image with some rather unfortunate history. The brutal boxing scene from Ralph Ellison's *Invisible Man* in which young boys pummel each other bloody for the diversion of inebriated patrons at a private gentleman's club is a far cry from the dynamic of college basketball. But one can imagine conference overseers concluding that it might be a good idea to expand the pool of minority referees, just to eliminate any doubts.

A related concern had to do with equal opportunity. Organized sports take justifiable pride in behaving as a living demonstration of meritocracy in action. True, there was some unpleasantness in pre–Jackie Robinson baseball and some duplicity in the years before Texas Western with its all-black starting five won the NCAA basketball tourney. But sports in general, and basketball in particular, have in recent decades evolved into a shining example of race-blind, merit-based selection, at least as it applies to the athletes who get the most playing time. Why not the same for referees?

To evaluate whether young Ed Hightower could handle tough situations, John Overby was dispatched by Herm Rohrig to Hutchinson, Kansas, where Hightower was slated to work the junior college championship game between San Jacinto College and Seminole State. Before the game even began, Overby detected a problem. Hightower wore eyeglasses. The verbal taunts that would soon spew from angered fans were not difficult to predict. Overby could almost hear them.

"You four-eyed black sonofabitch" would, in Overby's estimation, be the prevailing one, augmented by nastier embellishments as time went on.

As the game progressed, Overby grew to admire how Hightower comported himself, his self-assuredness and hustle, how he dashed to the right spot on the court, how he communicated with the coaches and took control of minor disputes between players. Overby was almost gleeful to behold such a pure display of raw referee talent. After the game, he informed Hightower that he was fully prepared to offer him assignments, starting next season, in the Missouri Valley Conference, which included such powerhouse programs as Indiana State, Southern Illinois, New Mexico State, and Creighton.

"But you've got to get rid of those horn-rims," Overby insisted.

He worried that Hightower might take umbrage, that he might be too stubborn or proud to acknowledge the unpleasant reality that fans were going to be rough on him, maybe rougher than they'd be on a white ref. He worried that Hightower might be the sort to get prickly at any suggestion that he alter his natural self simply to placate the mean-spirited impulses of rabid basketball fans.

On the other hand, Overby knew firsthand that perceived doubts based on appearance can harden a man's resolve to succeed. At 5'7", 150 pounds, he was told when he began refereeing that he would never make it because he was too small and would therefore never gain the aura of authority needed to manage a game. Bobby Knight repeatedly put Overby to the test. In one game, Overby slapped Knight with three technicals and banned him from the court. When Knight refused to leave, Overby summoned security police to escort Knight to the locker room. "Being short just made me work harder," he said.

When Overby next encountered Hightower, at his Missouri Valley Conference debut the following season, Hightower was without the eyeglasses, having switched to contact lenses. "It pleased the devil out of me," Overby recalled.

Hightower's career soon took flight. The year after breaking in with the Missouri Valley Conference, he was being assigned to Big Ten games. Five years later, he was working the Final Four. Over the ensuing nineteen years, he worked eleven more Final Fours, including four national championship games (Kansas vs. Oklahoma, 1988; UNLV vs. Duke, 1990; Michigan vs. UNC, 1993; Memphis vs. Kansas, 2008).

He was selected to work the 1990 World Championship basketball tournament in Argentina, the 1993 European Basketball Championship in Germany, and the 1994 Goodwill Games in St. Petersburg, Russia. Each of these was a long, improbable journey from Gobler.

He was named the Naismith Men's Collegiate Basketball Official of the Year (1992) and was recipient of the National Association of Sports Officials annual Gold Whistle award (1995).

He was invited to consider an NBA career but declined; it would mean surrendering his career in education. There too he'd made great strides. When he first started reffing, he was an assistant principal at Alton Junior High. He was next appointed assistant principal at Alton High. Then he became the principal, where he finally enjoyed the chance to occupy *for real* the very office where his fantasies of a career had first begun to germinate.

After enrolling in the PhD program at St. Louis University's College of Education, he was named assistant superintendent of Alton Schools. As he worked toward his doctorate, he was growing increasingly in demand as a ref. Life got very busy. Officiating as many as four games a week, he would arrive in Milwaukee or Ann Arbor or South Bend late afternoon, devour a hasty room-service meal while hunched over his thesis research binder. After the game, he'd return promptly to his hotel room to squeeze in another hour. Thesis topic: academic and social implications of tutorial programs on at-risk children in urban elementary schools. Thesis summary: "There is no reason every at-risk student should not have a tutor or, perhaps be a tutor. Not every tutor will be perfect, and not every program will reach all at-risk children equally well, but some form of effective tutoring is within the reach of every school district, no matter how small its resources."

In 1998, he became Edwardsville's superintendent of schools. Under Hightower's leadership — a vigorous, visionary, entrepreneurial style of leadership that Rick Pitino, Mike Krzyzewski, John Calipari, and even Bobby Knight would heartily applaud if public education was their thing — Edwardsville's schools consistently ranked among the best in Illinois. With 7,600 students, a 96 percent high school graduation rate, and 64 percent of the graduates moving on to four-year colleges, his day job keeps him busy. In 2001, he was named to the board of trustees of Southern Illinois University–Edwardsville, his alma mater.

He had innate talent, if such a thing exists in the realm of refereeing, and worked hard to hone his skills. Along the way he'd got his chance, and proved he was willing to work hard to make the most of it. Uplifting accounts of athletic heroes, from Lou Gehrig to Chris Paul, invariably cite these very factors.

Another recurring element in inspirational sports biographies: the hero humbly acknowledges, often with a self-effacing anecdote, that for all his achievements there were a few occasions where, but for fortune, it all might have gone south.

First time on national TV. Iowa versus Michigan State. Five seconds left on the game clock. The crowd is on its feet. Iowa brings the ball downcourt, trailing by two. This is crunch time, the very essence of it. The pass from Carfino as he skirts the sideline hits Hansen on the wing. Immediately, he shoots . . .

But it all worked out.

TOTAL QUALITY CONTROL

There's never been a perfectly refereed college basketball game, and there never will be. With the possible exception of a baseball pitcher's vaunted "perfect game," team sports do not lend themselves to such gemlike paragons of performance. Hank Nichols, who served as NCAA supervisor of officials for twenty-two years and is the only college basketball referee to have been inducted into the Basketball Hall of Fame, does, however, have a vision of what that imaginary perfect game might, from the beleaguered referees' perspective, consist of: "Both teams play zone defense," he quipped, "and the offense makes every shot."

Moments of clear-cut vindication, like Hightower's nullification of that final three-pointer in Iowa City, are the refs' equivalent of a game-winning shot, and they occur every bit as infrequently. The lion's share of officiating is spent without fanfare, without, if all goes well, any attention whatsoever. In stark contrast to the typical player's dream of getting showered with boisterous applause, it is the referee's wish to be met only with respectful silence or maybe a handshake afterward from the losing coach. A ref's game is spent methodically, painstakingly establishing boundaries, play by play by play, making the calls that are necessary to manage the flow and maintain fairness. It's a far better game if those calls are indisputably correct.

Coaches know that. Players know that. And so do the NCAA and the major conferences that make a surprisingly large investment of time and resources in the quality control of officiating. The unfathomable x factor may be real. The ability to instantaneously cut through the chaos may be innate. But there's plenty that can be observed, and quantified, and measured.

The more I watched Hightower in action and viewed the morass of intangibles that referees confront, the more I was struck by the many different ways there are to get it wrong (not that he does), and the many ways there are to be *proven* wrong (not that he often is). Attaching an asterisk to all but the most clear-cut calls would almost seem more forthright.

Psychologist Dan Simons, who is also engaged in a research project focusing on soccer officiating and analyzing the factors that contribute to a mistaken call (physical distance from play, divided attention), believes that referees periodically are called on to make decisions that encompass more visual information than they can adequately process in real time. Simons offered an example from baseball, the call that must be made on a runner being thrown out at first base: "There are three events occurring simultaneously at slightly different locations, and umpires must perceive all three. Has the runner's foot touched the bag? Is the first baseman's foot on the base? When did the ball hit the glove? You've got to know, did the runner's foot hit the bag before the ball hit the glove? Doing that requires split-second timing, paying attention to two things that aren't in the same location. It's remarkably hard."

Basketball referees, Simons explained, are often in comparably complex predicaments, when confronting the block/charge call, for example. "And the refs [unlike baseball umpires] are often running while doing this," he added.

Fifteen thousand fans shouting with blood-curdling fervor, the bedlam approaching "can't hear yourself think" decibel levels. On the court, ten pumped-up athletes jostle, veer, cut, slap, swirl, poke, spin, stumble, leap, and dive. Stuff happens, some of it intentional, some the result of honest accident. The line between right and wrong, permissible and not, is as slippery as liquid mercury spilled from a broken thermometer. How to determine amid a blurred frenzy of sensory distractions that what you *think you saw* is, in fact, *what you saw*? And how then to decide, with no additional delay, that what was seen merits your intervention?

I pressed Hightower and others to explain to me in layman's terms exactly what it takes to instantaneously gather such a vast array of visual data, simultaneously contextualize it, and then swiftly render a judgment that is unequivocal and assured.

Privately, I was continuing to chew over this notion that a referee's accumulated wisdom represents something special, even unique, with at least as much instructive value for us noncombatants as are allegedly contained in the countless parables spun from athletic and coaching glory. The quest to create order and achieve fairness in a hypercompetitive environment struck me as fertile soil for producing worthy insights, with widespread benefits. The very methods by which this quest for order and fairness was pursued, and the array of split-second judgments required to make it work, were, or so I told myself, potentially a valuable commodity with broad application to ordinary everyday functions.

Selling a call? A perfect concept to be used by elected officials, management consultants, parents.

Taking ownership of the play? Essential for sales managers, stock brokers, CEOs.

Whistle patience? Indispensable for civil engineers, venture capitalists, parents.

Mindfulness of whistle consequence? Just what the doctor ordered for prosecutors, newspaper editors, therapists, parents again.

An "Idiot's Guide to Decision Making under Pressure" was sort of what I had in mind, an everyday primer for the common man who'll never wear the zebra jersey. Who wouldn't benefit from honing an ability to be clear-eyed and decisive (and correct!) amid turbulent conditions? What I'd imagined was a package of carefully delineated, easy-to-follow steps (Five Steps, Seven Steps, whatever!) condensed in a format similar to what's found in popular, cleverly illustrated guides to, say, finding your perfect mate.

Hightower was of little help. You'd have thought I was asking a fish how it learned to swim. A ref's ability to cut through the chaos to discern essential truths, an acumen so potentially valuable to so many, was not a topic on which he was prepared to be analytical or reflective. It was a reprise of the frustrations in discussing the get-it factor. He got it. I couldn't.

Hank Nichols, another career educator, a former dean of education at Villanova, shrugged off my inquiry with the insouciance of Kevin Durant holding a postgame press conference in which he allowed that his forty-three-point outing was nothing more than one of those fortunate nights when his shot happened to be falling. "You just have to be able to do it," was as close as Nichols came to an explanation.

These refs' apparent inability to articulate precisely the intricate processes demanded by their craft struck me, curiously, as perhaps another aspect of the invisible gorilla syndrome. The act of concentrating with such ferocity on getting each call right consumed them completely, and required their complete attention. They had little cognitive capacity to spare for distinctly secondary questions, as they saw it, concerning how they were able to get it right. It was a question in my foreground but nowhere close to theirs.

Referee Jamie Luckie reported that he practices a three-stage mental-discipline technique that he's found to be useful. First, observe the play. Second, take a mental photograph of the play. Third, decide: whistle or no whistle. This process can consume no more than half a second. "Like clapping three times." He smacked his hands crisply to illustrate the precision, "Play, picture, decision."

OK, finally some headway. I asked Luckie if that methodology could be parsed into simple instructions for the lay population. "Can you actually teach that?"

Luckie shook his head apologetically. "I really don't know."

You'd never guess from all the accusations hurled from grandstands about their incompetence that referees in top-flight college basketball conferences are subjected to an extraordinarily rigorous evaluation process. Nearly every call and every significant non-call they make during the season — yes, during the *entire* season — is reviewed, analyzed, and graded. Each game is evaluated by an observer assigned by league supervisors to watch it in person or on TV. The observer records each call and notes its apparent validity, on a 1, 2, or 3 basis as though it were a middle school history essay (not, it should be added, as though it were a math test with cut-and-dried, right-wrong answers). After each game, league officials review the video of the game for the same purpose.

Within twenty-four hours after each game, each referee must complete and submit to the league a confidential evaluation concerning the performance of his two partners. Within forty-eight hours after the game, an online video file is created for the officials to access. These video clips are selected by an administrator at the conference headquarters or the supervisor of officials, and are meant to direct the recipient refs' attention to calls that the conference wants reviewed. Typically, there are between ten and fifteen of these per game. In addition, the NCAA rigorously evaluates the refs during each tournament game, and these evaluations play a vital role in which refs move forward in their separate yet parallel quest to make it to the Final Four. Each call is subjected to a pass-fail grade (correct/incorrect), and the refs are issued a "report card" after the game in which their individual whistles are identified by the nature of the call (HORB — hit on rebound, RPP — rough post play, TMC — too much contact, HOS — hit on shot, IS — illegal screen, OTB — over the back, etc.) and time-coded so the sequence can be easily reviewed on the accompanying video file.

At the end of each game, the referee receives an aggregate grade, "100" being perfect. Refs are entitled to contest their evaluations, and sometimes they do. Hightower told of a recent instance where a Big Ten supervisor, in his annotation to the online video of an Illinois-Nebraska game, had questioned a flagrant 1 foul Hightower had called on an Illinois breakaway near the end of game ("flagrant 1" being a recent replacement for an "intentional" foul, penalized by awarding the victimized team two free throws plus possession of the ball).

Hightower responded, via e-mail, that he felt Illinois had a clear path to the hoop and, if allowed to score, would have put the game away. On further review, the supervisor saw it the way Hightower had called it. Not all complaints get settled in the referees' favor. Here the ref is just another plaintiff hoping for a fair hearing.

Some may find it ironic that such subjective assessments (Was the call right, wrong, or justified? Was it a 1, 2, or 3? Was the ref's aggregate score for the game a 90, or an 85?) are superimposed on the necessarily subjective judgments (block or charge? over the back? in the act of shooting?) referees must make in the performance of their duties. Ironic perhaps, but an indispensable part of the quality-control process.

Plenty of vocations insist on rigorous assessment of their practitioners — and should. Doctors, teachers, lawyers, firefighters, social workers, and others mandate stringent standards for maintaining professional credibility. Many professions — police, nursing, aviation — systematically test and assess to make certain their personnel are equipped for the challenges ahead. But there are few, if any, professions in which people already successful in the field are scrutinized so closely *while* they perform, each time they perform.

Such scrutiny will only intensify as new technologies become available. In a move with likely repercussions for college basketball officials, the NBA recently announced it would begin employing sophisticated, six-camera data-tracking systems to monitor its referees. The SportVU systems can follow the movements of all ten players, all three refs, plus the ball, and do so in twenty-five-frames-per-second high-definition video. In effect, it can track every moment on the hardwood all the time. It will enable the NBA to grade each on-court official based on how consistently and early he gets into position and whether the calls made from these positions are appropriate, given the ref's sight lines. The NBA has already started using the cameras to check on such previously problematic areas as the enforcement of defensive three-second violations (defensive players lingering too long in the lane can be difficult to monitor for refs surveying other activities).

"We will use whatever data and means we can to improve our referees," declared Steve Hellmuth, the NBA's executive vice president of operations and technology. "The refs haven't been tracked before. Now for the first time, they will be."

As is the case with nearly all athletic activities, newer metrics are creeping into the discussion of officials. StatSheet, the artificial intelligence platform that logs trends in sports statistics, now tracks "leaders" in such categories as technicals called (43 in an 86 game schedule for Doug Simons), most fouls called per game (Brent Dugas with 43.5 for 2013–14), fewest fouls called per game (33.2), largest home team margin (–4.6); most blowout games called, most close games, most top-25 upsets called, most overtime games (Jamie Luckie with 10) and, perhaps of lesser import, most states visited.

The March Madness tournament, and the Final Four in particular, are assignments coveted by referees and granted on the basis of season-long evaluations. Refs compete to do the job well each night, and they compete to be recognized for excelling at it. Money is not the motivation. Compensation for officiating the NCAA tournament is substantially lower than for regular season games, usually about $1,000 per game including per diem for the first round. But the excitement of plying their craft at the epicenter of college basketball action and the secondhand glamor that attaches to that are sufficient reward. Greater still is the professional stature, and implied job security, this can bring. In 2011, Michael Stephens made his first ascent into the late rounds of the tournament, working a memorable Final Four matchup between Butler and Virginia Commonwealth. "Every national coach is there. They see you and it gives you credibility," he said. "It's like getting your wings."

Ninety-six refs are assigned at the outset of the NCAA tournament to work the opening round of thirty-two games. Following each game, the NCAA supervisor of officials and his team of assistants systematically evaluate the referees' performance. These ratings typically take the form of a "do not recommend," "recommend," or "strongly recommend" designation that will determine who gets promoted to each subsequent round.

Like the teams themselves, refs are thrilled each time they advance to a higher round, and conversely dejected on learning they're being thanked for their services, which will no longer be needed this season. In 2012, a writer for the website BleacherReport had the smart idea to itemize all the officials working the preliminary rounds of NCAA regional tournaments, noting their special attributes ("Brian O'Connell: Consistent in rules application and great court demeanor"; "Terry Wymer: Has excellent game-management skills and an even temper"; "Bryan Kersey:

Very good mechanics and great positioning"), and, in the spirit of pundits surveying the bracket lineups, he ventured a prediction as to which three refs would be selected to work the Big Game: Jamie Luckie, Les Jones, and Pat Driscoll.

The writer, after careful consideration of the likely candidates, failed to get a single one of them right. Which only goes to show just how tough these brackets can be.

. . .

To get a closer look at this evaluation process, I spent a game sitting courtside with Reggie Greenwood, a former Big Ten and Big East ref and currently the supervisor of officials for the Atlantic-10 Conference, the Patriot League, and the Ivy League. It was a late February matchup between LaSalle, a bubble team at that point in the season that eventually made it into the tournament and went all the way to the Sweet 16, and the University of Rhode Island, which was going nowhere. Outside, the weather was mercilessly awful, cold driving rain that periodically slashed down as sleet. Inside, it was cozy and warm.

Greenwood is a genial, imposing man with a neatly trimmed graying moustache and a strong resemblance to the actor Morgan Freeman. A former air traffic controller (another day job requiring skills that transfer well to reffing), Greenwood oversaw 245 refs across the three conferences for which he was responsible. Ten minutes before game time, he unpacked his professional tools and set them carefully atop the scorer's table. He had a laptop with several screens open to live feeds of games, an iPhone, and a legal pad with pages divided into the three vertical columns into which he would record, call by call, observation by observation, his evaluation of each of the three refs.

"Great toss," he exclaimed as Hightower, with but a moment's pause once the teams had assembled at mid-court, hoisted the ball into the air to begin the game.

The unremarkable toss-up would not have caught my eye. "It sets the tone," Greenwood explained.

Greenwood was particularly proud of the fact that in only his second season overseeing the Patriot League the visiting teams had won 53 percent of the games (statistical proof, of a sort, that his crews had resisted the influence of those noisy home-court atmospherics believed by the general public to subliminally affect a ref's judgment). Greenwood's rigorous evaluation takes several forms. He will have the DVD of each game reviewed. He will assign a neutral observer to monitor each game. Each of his refs is directed to report back on how the game went, including candid opinions on how each partner performed. He will ask both coaches to fill out a form grading each ref on a 1–5 scale in several categories: hustle and fitness; communication; judgment; attention to the rules; and consistency.

The game in Kingston was fast paced, with URI jumping out to an early, and as it turned out, unsustainable lead. Dan Hurley, the URI coach, was constantly hollering like a mad man and stomping up and down the sideline, well beyond the coach's designated boundaries. Greenwood was pleased that the refs, at least at this stage, ignored the infraction. "Why make it an issue if there's no impact?" he reasoned.

Two players got tangled over a loose ball, and the LaSalle player came up hobbling. No whistle. "Good no call," Greenwood remarked, citing the oft-employed RSBQ principle. "Rhythm, speed, balance, quickness. If it affects any of these, you need to put air in the whistle. If not . . ."

Refs are also judged on their ability to resist the lure of a valid, though unnecessary, call. I once sat with Rick Boyages, the Big Ten's associate commissioner and supervisor of officials, for a game between Northwestern and Baylor. Hunched over his laptop, much like Greenwood, Boyages was as consumed in typing out notes as a journalist attending a White House briefing. After each call, he hastily jotted a grade. On a breakaway layup by Baylor, a sprinting Northwestern defender reached out at the last instant, and made contact with the shooter's shoulder. Jim Burr, a veteran ref, blew his whistle. The shot fell through, unimpeded. Boyages was displeased. "Can't he just *not* call that? Can't he just *wait* a second to see what happens?"

Burr, it's worth noting, had worked sixteen Final Four's and seven national championship games. "Jim Burr is the best referee who ever lived," once gushed fellow ref Tim Higgins.

"Jim Burr is the worst ref of all time," opined a post on the Gamefaqs.com message board.

As the URI and LaSalle players swept swiftly back and forth, Greenwood was as attentive as a master choreographer to the precise positioning of his refs on the floor, what spots they ran to, what sight lines they maneuvered toward. Each of the three refs on the court, he pointed out, is simultaneously responsible for multiple levels of overlapping coverage: primary — their assigned sector of the court in the interlude prior to a field-goal attempt; secondary — the quickly revised configuration of players as a shot is released; tertiary — the further reshuffling as the rebound becomes the focal point of the action; quaternary — the transition as the defense takes possession of the ball. The degree of difficulty involved in efficiently accomplishing all of these nuanced repositionings brought to mind that cheesy handheld game, darling of birthday grab bags, wherein a child tries to tilt and slither several uncooperative BBs into an equal number of indented holes on a flat cardboard swatch. The challenge is getting each maddeningly mercurial little BB to stay put in its slot while shifting the angles in order to coax another one in. This proves especially frustrating while riding in a car. On a rough road with switchback turns.

As the LaSalle-URI game unfolded, Greenwood was a very busy

man. An air traffic control tower is no doubt a busier place, with far more at stake, than a basketball arena. By the same token, an air traffic control tower is probably more conducive to concentration. Courtside at the Ryan Center, Greenwood's phone buzzed incessantly. A call came in with game updates from a remote site. He showed me one text message he'd received earlier in the afternoon from a coach who will go unnamed. "Will send you clips of all the bullshit calls your crew made to fuck us today."

"Nowhere in that diatribe," Greenwood pointed out with droll understatement, "does he state, 'Oh, by the way, we turned the ball over twenty-two times.'"

Refs will ultimately be graded on the accuracy of their calls, or noncalls, ambiguous though the evidence may sometimes be. All systems have a need for metrics in their assessments. High scores = high quality.

To my eyes, much of this system of evaluation was hard to discern compared to the relative straightforwardness of other kinds of sports stats (shooting percentage, assist-to-turnover ratio) and I was reminded of Jamie Luckie's analogy to the scorekeeping in Olympic figure skating.

Clearly, there are aspects of officiating that do not neatly lend themselves to precise evaluation. Some crucial qualities, maybe *the* most crucial ones, may best flourish if they're unbridled, rather than regulated and tightly controlled. It's not that rules are, as the adage goes, meant to be broken. Rather, there are so darn many of them.

The men's basketball rules consume nearly 100 pages in the current NCAA rule book, covering nearly every imaginable contingency with finely wrought descriptive wording that valiantly attempts, as does the U.S. tax code, to leave no doubt. Take, for example, this definition of "closely guarded," a definition with significant implications for a variety of potential infractions: "A player in control of the ball in the front court only while holding or dribbling the ball is closely guarded when his opponent is in a guarding stance at a distance not exceeding 6 feet. This distance shall be measured from the forward foot or feet of the defender to the forward foot or feet of the opponent." Or this one pertaining to continuous possession: "Continuous motion applies to a try for field goal or free throw, but shall have no significance unless there is a foul by the defense during the interval that begins when the habitual throwing movement starts a try or with the touching on a tap and ends when the ball is clearly in flight."

Each rule is useful for its own distinct purpose. Each is a thoughtful response to styles of play or tactics that threaten to tarnish an idealized vision of how the sport should be fairly and optimally performed. As often happens, the profusion of rule refinements intended to preserve the essential spirit of the game can threaten to overwhelm their original purpose. They've become like an uninvited dinner guest who demands an outsized portion, plus impeccable service, and will not leave.

A strain of the old less-government-is-best-government philosophy can creep in. "Good officials don't care about the rule book," argued Digger Phelps, the former Notre Dame coach and current ESPN color commentator who admitted to wondering if the sport was better off in simpler times. "Shirts against skins worked pretty well," Digger asserted, perhaps overlooking the impact of crafty coaches, himself included, in provoking the need for greater regulation.

The 2012–13 season saw the average number of points scored per team, per game, in Division 1 (67.5) drop to the lowest level in thirty-one years. Not good. Not good for whom? Not good for the NCAA franchise. Can something be done, rule-wise, to reverse this trend? One plausible culprit: defenders getting away with too much benefit of the doubt on the block/charge call. Proposed corrective: a further refinement of the relevant rule. Starting the following season, the definition of "blocking" was adjusted to include any move by a defender into the path of the offensive player "once he has started his upward motion with the ball to attempt a field goal or pass." From the ref's perspective, this rule adjustment added an additional level of challenge to what was already a very tough call to make.

That said, the referee's task, like that of the police officer patrolling a stressful beat, is to enforce the laws, not to write them. And what refs tend to believe is what cops tend to know: laws are crucial to a civilized society, and the final decision as to when the whistle should be blown or when it's best to let it go should be left to them with their streetwise experience. If the goal is the establishment of a just and orderly environment, why not permit a little flexibility in administering rules?

This conundrum was wonderfully dramatized in Herman Melville's classic novella, *Billy Budd*. The story takes place in 1797 aboard a British Royal Navy ship riddled with tension. The HMS *Bellipotent* feared an attack by the French navy, and the ship's officers were on edge from reports of mutinies at sea on other ships. Billy Budd is a popular, virtuous young sailor who is mercilessly antagonized by John Claggart, the brutal master-at-arms. Claggart falsely accuses Billy of conspiring to mutiny. Infuriated and thwarted from verbally defending himself by an intense stutter, which Claggart had repeatedly mocked, Billy lashes out with a swift punch. Claggart topples backwards, cracking his skull on one of the ship's cannons, and is killed. Everyone on board, including the ship's captain, is of the opinion that Billy is essentially innocent, guilty of nothing more than justifiable self-defense. But the laws that govern ships at sea, in light of the extreme need for maximum order, are ironclad. "Struck dead by an Angel," decrees the captain. "Yet the Angel must hang!"

"The power of elasticity" or "elastic power" is the how this principle — or absence of it in the case of *Billy Budd* — is known to sports officials. It means that in certain situations the referee can turn the rulebook into something malleable, or render decisions that are not specifically covered in the rulebook. Where the rules are specific, there's no flexibility. Step out-of-bounds, play is dead. Where the rule requires judgment — incidental contact, for example — judgment is required to determine if the rule was violated. In its broadest sense, the concept of elasticity enables officials to occasionally employ common sense to override or temper strict adherence to the rulebook.

Referees don't make the rules and, like cops, they don't always agree with all of them. I'd heard their occasional grumblings about wishing they were empowered to exercise judgment more often, especially when it came to resorting to video review. "Good officials will find a reason to go to the monitor when they need to," observed Rich Falk, formerly of the Big Ten, by which he meant that within the strict guidelines for employing video review some real-time wiggle room could occasionally be created.

Similarly, Falk noted that a spontaneous eruption from a crowd can signal to a savvy ref, one with a connoisseur's ear, that something's amiss. Refs are inured to all manner of booing and cheering. They understand that wily coaches playing at home are forever trying to provoke their audience into making noise. But sometimes a spontaneous outburst from the crowd is a legitimate, authentic response to a call about which the ref already had some misgivings. An example of this occurred during an Indiana versus Northwestern game I watched with Falk.

A fight for the rebound under the basket sent the ball skittering out-of-bounds and it was awarded to Indiana, the visiting team. The crowd instantly let loose with a loud, prolonged choral howl, wholly impromptu. With the ball out-of-bounds, there was a moment to reflect, and the sustained anger from the grandstand gave

Hightower and his colleagues a moment to confer. The coaches fretted. The players meandered. The call was reversed. "People up in the stands, let's face it, sometimes have a better view of the play than we do," Falk explained.

This unstated license to employ elasticity on rare occasions, to be wise interpreters of what the laws are intended to accomplish, can entrust elite referees with something like emergency powers. It was not a practice for rookies. It was not a practice for the inexperienced or the spineless. Nor for robotic sensing devices. The power of elasticity was reserved for humans, and only for the most capable among them.

I mentioned *Billy Budd* to Hightower, not being sure if he knew the story (it was probably not part of Edwardsville's core curriculum, or that of many school districts). He had, as it turned out, a story of his own.

The game was the 2008 NCAA championship game, Memphis versus Kansas. Led by freshman phenom Derrick Rose, Memphis was up by two points. With sixteen seconds left in regulation time, Memphis's Chris Douglas-Roberts missed two consecutive free throws that might have effectively iced it for the Tigers. When a time-out was called several seconds later, Douglas-Roberts, upset with himself, grabbed the ball and angrily slammed it down. The ball rocketed fifteen feet above the court.

This fit of bad-boy petulance was precisely the kind of petty juvenile tantrum, acted out in front of the largest possible national viewership, that the NCAA was avid to crack down on. Gleeful at their impending good fortune, the Kansas bench and its battalion of assistant coaches immediately began yelling for a technical foul to be called.

Hightower was the lead ref in the game. He understood perfectly well that a technical was warranted. As much as any referee working the major conferences, he firmly believed these student-athletes suffered lasting personal harm through the myriad ways they'd been coddled and excused throughout their young lives, simply due to their remarkable basketball skills. Granting exceptions to star athletes for misbehavior was not Superintendent Hightower's style.

Moreover, he understood perfectly well that in the eyes of any by-the-book NCAA administrator who might review his performance, an emphatic, no-nonsense whistle was exactly what this transgression called for. The Memphis kid behaved like a brat. Slap him with a "T."

But this was the national championship game. Ten seconds remained on the clock. Douglas-Roberts had done something remarkably dumb. He'd done it in flagrant violation of the rules. In plain view of millions of viewers. But he was only a kid. And his stupid, self-indulgent act, showing off his disappointment by slamming the ball, had been, in the broader scheme, nothing worse than merely dumb.

Hightower retrieved the ball. He marched directly up to the 6'7" Douglas-Roberts. He fixed him with a stare of cold disapproval, and snapped, "*What* are you doing?"

It was a stern school principal's firm and final warning: grow up, show respect, play ball. No technical was called.

"It's not about the letter of the law," Hightower later explained. "What was the kid's intent? It wasn't to embarrass me. He was frustrated. He'd just missed a key free throw in the national championship game. You've got to understand the moment, and what's happening out there before you put air in the whistle."

Hightower steps in to restore peace in a clash between Purdue and Iowa. "The basketball arena is a very, very partisan place," said Hightower. "If fair and balanced is my goal, what are the chances of pleasing all 16,000 people?" *Photo by Brian Spurlock*

Wisconsin coach Bo Ryan has some advice for Hightower, who
has heard it all before. The relationship between college coaches
and referees working their games is one of the strangest imaginable,
fraught with simmering tension. *Photo by Mary Langenfeld, courtesy
of USA Today Sports*

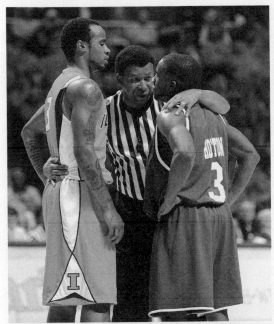

Dialing down the passions in a clash between Chicago State and Illinois. "Our job," explained J. D. Collins, a supervisor of officials, "is to absorb the chaos, create calm, and provide hope that the outcome will be fair."
Photo by Cary Frye

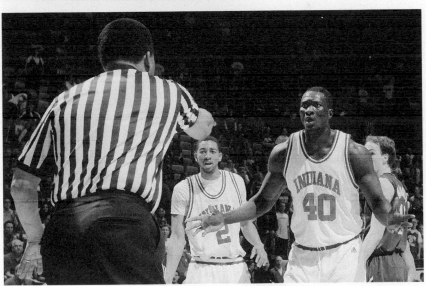

Referees need to reach a verdict swiftly and communicate it clearly. "You are there in order to render that final decision," Hightower said. "The quicker you make a decision, the better off for everybody." *Photo by James Brosher, courtesy of* Bloomington Herald Tribune

A rare moment of calm during a time-out at the 1993 Final Four. Hightower officiated twelve Final Fours and four NCAA championship games, including several nail-biting classics. *Photo by Brian Spurlock*

Hightower's mother, Daisy, pictured here in 1965 at age 30, ran a notoriously tight ship. "You know it when you are doing somebody right," she would sternly instruct her young children, including the future referee. "And you know it when you're doing somebody wrong." *Photo courtesy of Ed Hightower*

Edwardsville's schools have consistently been ranked among the best in Illinois as a direct result of Hightower's visionary, entrepreneurial tenure as school superintendent. *Photo by Caleb Motsinger*

In his office with a grade school student stricken by a rare blood disorder. It wasn't hard to see the overlap between his duties as school superintendent and as referee. *Photo courtesy of Ed Hightower*

By most accounts, Hightower is Edwardsville's MVP and has been for many consecutive seasons. Here he tosses candy to bystanders from the back of a convertible during the town's annual homecoming parade. *Photo by Tom Atwood, courtesy of Ed Hightower*

Instructional camp attendees gather to review what they've learned at the D3 Super Camp held at the University of Richmond. As pay has improved and the volume of telecasts has added to the luster, more aspiring refs are motivated to "take their game" to the next level. *Photo courtesy of D3 Super Camp*

Veteran ref Jamie Luckie preparing to put the ball in play. "Nobody's going to like you anyways," he tells novice refs at summer instructional camps, "so you might as well be right." *Photo courtesy of Jamie Luckie*

For the ref, video review is blessing and curse, a tool of immense value and an instrument of potential humiliation. Hightower (center) weighs the visual evidence along with colleagues John Hughes (on the left, facing the monitor) and Ray Perone. *Photo by Brian Spurlock*

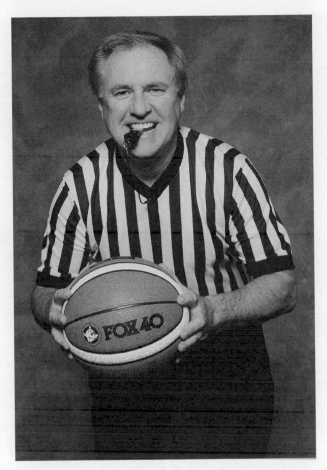

A whistle that does what's needed when it's needed is an official's one indispensable tool. Ron Foxcroft learned the hard way what can go wrong and invented the invaluable Fox 40 "pealess" whistle. *Photo courtesy of Ron Foxcroft*

A gutsy, last-second, game-deciding call on the final play, the ref's equivalent of a walk-off home run, would make for a fitting end to Hightower's career. *Photo by Brian Spurlock*

SCREENS FROM EVERY ANGLE

A few years ago, I attended the annual Big East Conference basket-
ball-referee clinic held at Villanova University, near Philadelphia.
Major Division 1 conferences hold these preseason sessions as a
kind of refresher course. The season just concluded had yielded
a trove of predicaments and fiascos that were ripe to be decon-
structed in the company of the only people on the planet capable of
understanding what actually had transpired. And the season about
to begin was already prompting the need for tweaks and adjust-
ments — new rules, revised interpretations of old rules, evolving
moves and techniques by tricky players that require adaptation.

Displayed along the high walls of Villanova's state-of-the-art
practice gym were several punchy slogans in bold print — Play
Hard, Play Together, Play Smart — reminiscent of state-sponsored
billboards you might see along Soviet Bloc highways back in the
day, extolling habits sure to increase productivity. The gym's var-
nished floor, with the morning sun streaming through its high
windows, glistened like a skating rink. Two long rows of folding
metal chairs had been set up along one sideline. It was quiet, peaceful, almost a place of contemplation.

The refs began arriving in the groups of three and four from
the nearby Marriott where they were staying. They greeted each
other warmly, like school kids reuniting after summer recess, and
immediately fell into merry clusters of conversation. Ranging
in age between thirty and sixty-six, they were a healthy-looking

group, although not, given their chosen athletic affiliation, notably tall. Their attire was country-club casual, the kind of classic-fit polo shirts in tropical pastel hues and pleated slacks that business executives might wear at a weekend barbecue hosted by a prized account.

The agenda for the two-day conference called for numerous instructional sessions as well as a golf outing. Not all referees are avid golfers, but many are and they do enjoy the easy joshing which that leisure-time sport so famously facilitates.

"How's the golf game?" Hightower was asked almost as soon as he arrived by a younger man who, with a deep tan and snappy casual dress, could pass for a PGA professional.

"It stinks," he laughed.

They mingled jovially, slapping hands with something less than the hip dexterity of the cool young dudes they referee, but cooler than most middle-aged golfers. With high-spirited humor, they traded quick digs on an assortment of topics, the late season nosedive of the Phillies, the trials of sticking to a meatless diet, Romney's polling numbers in Illinois. Gradually they began to take their seats, one by one. Class would soon be called to order. As they peeled away from their conversational clusters and headed down the line of chairs to find a vacant seat, they reflexively reached out to slap five with those already seated, like ballplayers returning to the dugout after scoring a run.

Gene Steratore was one of the later arrivals. Immediately on entering the gym, he was met with a flurry of congratulations that went beyond generic good cheer. Referees are an egalitarian lot. They spend enough time in the presence of self-important men with oversized egos to have cultivated a healthy skepticism of that particular human trait. In their on-court basketball responsibilities, labor is shared equally and success depends on helping each other out, watching each other's back. They are teammates in the fullest sense. Of course some are more privileged and more praised than others. Some refs receive preferred assignments. Some get selected for the year-end tournaments. But the dominant ethos is one-for-all, all-for-one.

Yet Steratore, it was clear, had catapulted into a special status. He was, I learned, also an NFL referee, the only official currently doing both, and therefore, at this time, early fall 2012, very much in the hot seat. Since the pro football season began several weeks earlier, pro officials had been locked out in a contentious labor dispute that had received prime-time media coverage. The plight of the football officials, locked out by billionaire owners over wage and benefit issues, and with their game-day responsibilities handed over to under-qualified scabs, had certainly captured the attention of these referees, and their sympathy. The labor dispute and the public reaction to it were of more than academic interest to this group.

Would the NFL players stand up in support of the veteran refs? Would the players voice concern over games being poorly officiated by unprepared rookies? Would the hard-charging head coaches protest the penalty-calling inconsistencies that were bound to emerge? Would fans notice the lack of decisiveness and the muddled communication of yellow-flag infractions? Would the time management of the games, so vital to the revenue flow from the television industry, be compromised? Would a decline in the officiating, accumulated over the course of enough games, jeopardize pro football's immense popularity?

Or would something alarmingly like the opposite be discovered, that quality officiating was more or less expandable? Or worse, would the increase in blown calls and attenuated controversies prove bizarrely to be a sideshow with box office appeal?

During the first weeks of September, such questions were being hotly debated across the sprawling sports media landscape. Basketball refs, along with officials in other sports, closely watched each development. The implications for their own situation were unmistakable. If the key stakeholders in professional football opted to compromise the quality of refereeing, as seemed to be the case with the lockout continuing, then it might finally be time for Hightower and his brethren to confront some unwelcome conclusions regarding how much, or little, their efforts were valued? The NFL labor struggle was, in effect, a proxy for larger issues, the fundamental one being: How important are the officials to the integrity of the game?

A swarthy, voluble, muscular man with the feisty air of Al Pacino in his prime, Steratore, along with his brother Tony, who is also an NFL ref, own a cleaning-product-supply business (mops, squeegees, chemical disinfectants, etc.) in Washington, Pennsylvania. Without reveling in the special attention, he graciously accepted the supportive comments and gestures of solidarity from his Big East reffing comrades.

Almost everyone attending this clinic had worked games with Steratore and had heard his views, ardent and articulate, about the similarities and differences between college basketball and pro football officiating. Basketball, he pointed out, required the refs to move fast and decide swiftly. Football, in contrast, contains a plethora of naturally occurring pauses (essentially between every play) that can seamlessly serve as occasions to deliberate. "In football," Steratore said, "our mantra is: when you think you're going slow, go slower."

Steratore was acutely aware of the pressure placed on college basketball refs by the tightly circumscribed conditions in which referees are permitted to confer with each other in a pinch and resort to the video monitor. In January 2012, he'd reffed a Syracuse–West Virginia game that ended 63–61, with West Virginia's final attempt at a game-tying shot being blocked by what many observers, including Dick Vitale and Jay Bilas of ESPN, believed to be an illegal goaltend. "I would've loved to be able to run over to Karl Hess," explained Steratore, referring to one of the other refs in that game, "and ask, what did you see? I would love to be able to confer the way we do in football."

Hightower sidled over to clap Steratore on the shoulder. They'd worked together numerous times and were familiar with the basics of each other's lives — family, upbringing, hobbies and social values, off-season vocations.

"You know, Gene," Hightower chided with a devilish smirk, "we really could use you at some Edwardsville High football games this fall. Hundred twenty-five, hundred fifty bucks per game? Plus gas mileage? Come on, what do you say?"

Hightower planted himself in the chair nearest the exit, in case he needed to step out to take a call. All the refs were familiar with his 24/7 school-district responsibilities, and had left this seat vacant for him as though it were a place of honor.

He wore a light blue long-sleeve dress shirt, dark slacks, and polished black shoes. No suit today, but with his Bluetooth wireless looped above his right ear, he was poised, should duty call, to be Dr. Hightower, Superintendent of Schools. The unceasing demands that his day job placed on him and his compulsive attention to his impatient phone were well known to his fellow refs. They rolled their eyes every time it rattled. Brian O'Connell, a Big East ref, claimed to have driven from St. Louis to Iowa City, a trip of four hours, with Hightower spending the entire journey on the phone. An exaggeration, no doubt. Yet believable.

There was a decided end-of-summer-recess mood in the Villanova practice gym. Once all the refs were, as teachers like to say, settled in their seats and quietly facing forward, Art Hyland, head of the Big East officials and rules interpreter for NCAA basketball, stepped to center court. Slightly rumpled in creaseless chinos, a loose red sport shirt with the collar poking up irregularly, and sneakers so scuffed and worn they could almost pass as bedroom slippers, Hyland called the class to order.

Villanova coach Jay Wright was the first presenter. His subject would be off-the-ball screens. A strikingly handsome man, Wright is often likened to George Clooney. Frequently named to GQ magazine's "Fashionable Four" — hey, why shouldn't college coaches get recognized for achievements besides basketball success? — Wright made a point of dressing down for this occasion. He sported a blue Villanova athletic shirt that hung loose over his blue basketball shorts.

Wright began with a synopsis of things referees should understand about coaches.

"We're out of our minds during games," he stated without apology. "But no matter how much we argue and complain, 99 percent of the time when we go back and watch the tape afterward, we see what you see. And even when you don't get it right, we see why you made the call."

An olive branch, to be sure. The refs nodded their approval. And a minute later they were chuckling with approval as Wright referenced an anecdote, familiar to many refs because it had been recounted by Hank Nichols in his recent acceptance speech on being inducted into the Basketball Hall of Fame in Springfield, Massachusetts. Nichols had a run-in, so the story goes, with the fiery former University of Maryland coach Lefty Driesell. After a game in which Lefty was more than typically disgruntled over the officiating, he meticulously assembled an annotated videotape of ten calls he accused Nichols of getting dead wrong during the game, and express-mailed the tape to the Atlantic Coast Conference headquarters. He demanded that the league review the evidence and own up to what it revealed. After reviewing the tape, the league concluded that Nichols in fact got each of the disputed calls correct.

"Well, he might have gotten them right on film," Lefty reputedly fulminated, "but he sure as hell missed them in the damn game!"

That was a bygone era, Wright seemed to be suggesting with a wink, when refs were treated with knee-jerk enmity and coaches were reflexively antagonistic as well as unenlightened. The implication was that contemporary coaches, present company very much included, understood how difficult it was to officiate these games and they appreciated the fact that the refs mostly get it right.

Except, perhaps, when the coaches get crazy.

Coach Wright, standing at center court, was as masterful as a corporate trainer. The Villanova practice gym's gleaming hardwood was his home turf rehearsal space, and he was *very* comfortable with the material.

Wright placed a hand on the shoulder of an assistant and guided him like a chess piece to a spot on the floor. He did the same with another assistant, positioning him a few yards away. He then summoned another aide, this one his videographer, and told him to dribble the ball along a prescribed path. He wanted the referees to see what coaches are hoping to achieve with different configurations of the multiplayer screen.

"This type of screen is getting popular," he said of a maneuver he labeled a "step-up screen." "It's used a lot in the NBA."

Wright then realigned his human pawns, and instructed the videographer to dribble at a different angle of intersection. "Flat ball screen. It's the most difficult for us to defend. And probably the most difficult for you to call." Why? Because, I was later told, when contact results from the offensive and defensive players moving simultaneously in the same direction, it's so hard to determine which player has gained an advantage.

at the precise frame where the breakaway pass was initiated. Over and over, subdividing what could not have added up to more than five or six seconds of real-time action, this fellow carefully studied each brief segment with a hyper-attention befitting a crime-scene detective. What was so darn fascinating?

He kept at it until the intercom informed us that we were entering our descent to Chicago's O'Hare Airport and everyone should . . . to their upright and locked positions.

I couldn't resist. After the plane landed, I approached him with what I believed sounded like a polite disclaimer, "Excuse me, I couldn't help but notice . . ."

He was an NBA referee. The tape was from a game he'd worked earlier in the week.

I didn't want to appear too nosy, so I refrained from asking who the teams were and who had won. But I did want to know why he was scrutinizing this snippet as though it was the crucial seconds of the Zapruder film.

He told me he was interested as to how the player who'd broken away for the uncontested layup had managed to become so alone and unguarded so quickly. He was puzzled how the play had developed and he suspected a subterfuge, of a possibly illegal nature, perhaps a detaining tug on a jersey or some other sly form of interference.

"Did you find what you were looking for?"

He wouldn't say. But his self-satisfied expression suggested he did.

The large number of topics crammed into the Big East ref clinic would be familiar to anyone who's ever attended for-credit professional development seminars, at least those that are not thinly disguised golf-outing boondoggles in Vegas or Orlando. Topics included: Trail Ref Responsibilities; Refereeing Shots from the

Corner; Restricted Arc Coverage; Reporting of Fouls to Scorer and to Coaches; Principles and Monitoring of the Block/Charge; Use of the Monitor for Correctable Errors; Stop Clock Guidelines Regarding Injuries on Offense and Defense; Held Ball Plays; and more.

Each of these mini-refresher courses was conducted by one of the refs, and embellished by Hyland's Socratic observations.

"What do you do about a zone?" Hyland interrupted Evon Burroughs, a Boston police officer, as he was holding forth on the topic of "rotations." "You can't keep going back and forth all the time. It'd be like a yo-yo."

Hyland, a Cape Cod attorney and former Princeton star who played alongside Bill Bradley in an era that's preserved mostly in black-and-white photos, presided over each session with a gruff bemusement. He did not say much, but when he did it carried the compounded impact of being on-target and coming from someone with the authority to do something about it. In addition to being the Big East's supervisor of officials, he sat on the NCAA basketball rules committee.

During the session on "Refereeing Screens," he interjected, "If we call an illegal screen, they need to be obvious because we're taking a possession away."

During a discussion of positioning on the court ("Ninety percent of the time we miss a call it's because we're in the wrong position by only two feet," according to J. D. Collins, a coordinator of officials for the Mid-American and Summit Leagues) Hyland interrupted to note, "I get scared when I see the sideline ref coming out onto the court. I don't know why you think you can see more by moving out onto the floor. Looks to me like a disaster waiting to happen."

Hightower's phone rattled midway through the session on "Officials Jurisdiction re Safety, TV Equipment, and Fan Issues," and he scooted away to take the call in the foyer. If there were an Olympic competition for multitasking effectively without any semblance of annoyance or losing composure, Hightower could be one of the favorites. I've seen him wrestle with a stressful school department issue on his iPhone while negotiating a crowded interstate at high speeds in a driving rain, and then, deftly swerving lanes to gain an edge on the trio of tractor-trailers impeding him from increasing his speed — maybe, an additional two miles per hour — switch to a call from the St. Louis hospital nurse who'd been instructed, by him, to phone anytime, day or night, that his mother's condition (she was hospitalized for a heart-related problem) worsened or improved, and then *place* a call via voice-activated autodial to a school superintendent in a neighboring town who wanted a reference on a prospective job candidate.

I was with him once in Madison Square Garden, in the referee's distinctly un-lavish utility closet of a locker room before the start of a game. He was massaging a mentholated muscle gel deep into his calf and thigh muscles, as he does before every game, and took a call from Edwardsville.

"He did *what*?" Hightower does not easily register alarm.

He listened intently, rubbing the menthol gel into his upper arms and shoulders.

"Were there any witnesses?"

Pause.

"Were the witnesses black or white?"

Longer pause.

"Got it. Were there any cameras?"

"Cameras not working? That's unacceptable!"

I learned later what had been involved. A bus driver on an after-school route got into a tiff with a student who had reportedly called the driver "a fucking nigger." The student was second-generation European American. That hardly constituted a mitigating circumstance, in Hightower's estimation.

"Five-day suspension," he snapped without hesitation. "Minimum. And tell his mother: this happens again, we'll find another place for him."

Case closed, Hightower removed his Blackberry earpiece, carefully placed it into his locker, and headed down the dingy hallway and then out to the bright lights of Madison Square Garden to work what promised to be a rugged Cincinnati–St. John's contest.

Tough calls made swiftly and decisively are Hightower's stock-in-trade. As superintendent, they come at him with alarming regularity, from every angle, without warning.

A father phones to complain that his son's locker was unfairly targeted by drug-sniffing dogs from the Edwardsville Police Department. The student's locker had indeed been sniffed out by the dogs, but the police search of his locker came up empty. Still, the boy's parents persisted in accusing the school department, and at one point demanded that all such canine searches be suspended. Hightower's response: the parents should be pleased that nothing incriminating was discovered. End of discussion.

The mother of a talented high school basketball player who is considering relocating to the Edwardsville district wants assurances from the coach, the principal, and the superintendent that her son will get varsity playing time as a freshman. On this one, Hightower showed no whistle patience whatsoever: her request to speak with the boys' basketball coach and the principal was summarily denied. The boy enrolled at another high school, where he was a starter all four years. He went on to play for Butler.

A hard-won private grant intended to establish a model program for underperforming, at-risk students is scuttled on the very day it's set to be awarded because the corporate official overseeing the process was suddenly charged with embezzlement. This one stings. But a bad call at the final buzzer is not, in this instance, reviewable.

Parents and community leaders flood into the Woodland Elementary auditorium on a warm August evening. Outside, two hundred protesting teachers hoist placards proclaiming "Fairness Is All We Ask." For two hours, Hightower is besieged by complaints from those opposing any tax increase and those opposing any cuts in teacher pay. Shared sacrifice, he states in conclusion, is the only option. Few are happy.

The crossover to his responsibilities on the hardwood court is not hard to fathom. On average, he may be involved in making some twenty-five calls per game. Some are obvious, others not. Among coaches and refs, there's no consensus as to which calls are toughest. Goaltending is often cited. Also the block/charge. Rick Pitino believes the over-the-back foul is the most difficult to get right; he likens it to the nebulous, often subjective infraction of holding by an offensive lineman in football. Rich Falk, the former Northwestern coach and Big Ten supervisor of officials, points to incidental contact, the crashing of bodies or colliding of limbs that does not produce a discernible advantage or disadvantage for either player. "Incidental contact," Falk argues, "separates the men from the boys."

It is this shared experience of making tough calls, in the spotlight, under pressure, clock ticking relentlessly down, that binds refs together and shapes them into something resembling a cult. There is a general feeling among them that the pressures and pitfalls they endure can be fully appreciated only by other refs. The very nature of their assignment sets them apart from other stakeholders — players, coaches, media, fans. This "outsider" status is accentuated by a slew of insider points of reference and an in-crowd vocabulary that goes with it.

Angle screen, wing screen, hedge screen. Each time Jay Wright reshuffled his chess-piece assistants to illustrate yet another confounding (to me) configuration, he called out its designation. This was a graduate-level seminar, meant for parties who already possessed a sophisticated knowledge of the subject matter. *Blarge* (a ref-speak contraction denoting the block-charge dilemma), *verticality, pass/crash, incidental contact.* This vernacular, known primarily to seasoned practitioners, coaches included, was their secret handshake, strengthening their bond.

I never got the sense that the refs were learning anything particularly new in these sessions. You don't get to an elite level like the Big East Conference without mastering such intricacies, and putting them into practice in numerous pressure-packed games. With the exception of a few directives pertaining to updated guidelines — against the swinging of elbows, for example — most of the material was standard refresher course fare, intended, in anticipation of the long upcoming season, to prod them back into focusing on the challenges ahead.

The high-ceilinged Villanova gym, bathed in sunlight, was silent except for the single echoing voice of whoever was speaking. For the referees, the church-like tranquility of this gym would soon give way to a mammoth arena. Soon, the arena would be filled with screaming wackos. Soon, every whistle, every snap judgment, would have repercussions. The coaches would be watching. Soon, it would get serious.

It hardly needed to be said.

"Good luck," Hyland cheerfully declared in closing the session, and it struck me that this throwaway phrase held actual meaning. Referees, like the athletes, are players in this game. Luck can indeed prove to be a factor. All the better if it's good.

. . .

There's one Hightower game among the many that I really wish I had seen in person. It was a wintry Saturday afternoon in February 1984, DePaul versus Notre Dame. Hightower had managed to arrive in South Bend by late morning but his two colleagues unfortunately had not. Delayed in Decatur, Illinois, by fog, Jim Bain and Ralph Rosser were able to secure a private plane to get there, only to have its propeller damaged while it was being towed to the runway. The prop was finally repaired, but the plane's vacuum pump broke before takeoff. A second private plane was obtained but by this time it was clear the refs would not make it to South Bend in time. If all went well, they expected to arrive at the Joyce Center about twenty minutes after the scheduled start of the contest. Delay the tip-off? No way, said NBC, which was broadcasting the game.

There was a plan B. Two local high school referees, presumed to be competent, were in attendance. Learning of the dilemma, they'd come courtside to offer their services. To Hightower, using these substitute refs for an abbreviated interlude seemed an imperfect yet acceptable solution. He would have to assume a greatly enlarged role and be willing to exercise veto power over any of their less expert calls. But better that than nothing.

Ray Meyer, the wily seventy-year-old DePaul coach (and a living piece of basketball history for having coached George Mikan, the game's first dominant big man) did not like the idea one bit. Inexperienced refs, in his opinion, would be too susceptible to the bullying tactics of his rival coach. Digger Phelps, the irascible Notre Dame coach, felt the same way for the same reason.

The only alternative was to compel Ed Hightower, in only his second season in the big leagues, to fly solo in what was sure to be a hard-fought game (DePaul, with a 16–1 record, was ranked no. 2 in the nation). This seemed like pure folly. But that was the decision.

For nearly five minutes, Hightower was the lead, trail, and center official, a one-man triangle. His approach was to restrict his range of movement to the condensed territory between the respective free throw circles, and try to remain on only one side of the court. That left a whole lot of real estate consigned to be less closely monitored than normal. Even under ideal three-ref conditions, things often went unseen. Players were always sneaking an unfair advantage if they thought they could get away with it. What sneaky tricks would they try to get away with now?

Hightower worried about all that might get overlooked, and was particularly worried, despite their friendly pledges, about the skullduggery of the two notoriously shrewd coaches. They'd indicated that they might lay back a bit, but he expected the carping would surface at some point, if only to test him. As for the packed house of partisan Notre Dame fans, well, as long as they did not hurl hard objects that succeeded in hitting their target, he'd ignore their taunts. That phase of his game could remain the same.

Astonishingly, it did not happen that way. Every call he made was met with polite silence. The players acted like Boy Scouts, obediently raising their hands when called for an infraction, fetching the ball for him when he needed to put it back in play, resisting the temptation to deceive him into a false whistle. The Fighting Irish fans acted as respectfully as though this were a commencement ceremony rather than a bitter showdown against a heavily favored Catholic university rival. Sure, they cheered their home team hoops and groaned when DePaul came right back to score, but they refrained from the usual assortment of howled epithets and choral harassment. It took a couple of minutes for Hightower to cue in to what was actually taking place.

Not only was this *not* torture, it was quite possibly something miraculous and wonderful.

Try to imagine it: a tense college basketball clash with barnburner fervor and nobody was ragging on the ref. You would hear the sharp squeak of sneakers scuffing the hardwood. You'd hear the heartbeat thumping of the dribbled ball. The crowd would grow boisterous after a brilliant play and that happy squeal of shared elation was all you heard. Ray Meyer chewed out a defender who'd failed to block out on a rebound, but had nothing but pleasant nods of approval for Hightower. Digger had no complaints either. It was as if he'd been dosed with lithium.

It was all like a beautiful dream. Wake me when it's over.

With 15:14 left in the first half, the two tardy refs finally arrived. No sooner did Hightower resume, with immense relief, his standard practice of patrolling the court as one point of a flexible triangle, than the players and coaches and fans reverted to *their* standard behavior. Players proclaimed their innocence of every whistle directed their way. One coach or the other, or both, carped and scowled at nearly every call. A mood of harmony was replaced with one of barely concealed malevolence. Dream over. Game on!

"The two guys who were late should've stayed home," Digger complained afterward.

THE PARADOX OF VIDEO REVIEW

Let's face it: Much of what fans know, or think they know, about sports officials derives from the experience of watching video replays. Those prolonged TV time-out interludes in which an official judgment on a controversial play is painstakingly examined and re-examined, X-rayed from different angles and held high to the light for all to see, are fundamental to our appraisal of the capabilities of referees. Tough calls by refs in crucial situations have forever sparked disputes. But it's video replay, and the aura of certainty it encourages in skeptical fans, that's truly fanned the flames.

It was not always thus.

George Retzlaff, a Toronto-based producer for the Canadian Broadcasting Corporation's popular *Hockey Night in Canada* is credited with first introducing a rudimentary form of video replay in the mid-1950s (the CBC once ranked this development no. 24 on its list of the greatest Canadian inventions of all time). A few years later, Tony Verna, a director at CBS who'd experimented with videotape while working the 1960 Rome Olympics, began using replay during professional football telecasts to fill the lulls between snaps and during injury delays. It soon became clear that this technique contained almost magical powers to illuminate what had actually occurred on plays where the real-time, one-take, field-level visual perspective, which is to say the only perspective available to the referees and umpires tasked with rendering a definitive judgment, was muddled or plain wrong.

Suddenly the sports world's traditional reliance on the eyesight and discernment of officials could be augmented by a technological backup option with the power to correct or compensate for human deficiencies. The jury (or was it the judge?) could now request to review the evidence before coming to a final conclusion.

On April 17, 1977, during a baseball game in Atlanta between the Braves and the Houston Astros, the operator of the Atlanta-Fulton County Stadium scoreboard in center field, which had been recently modernized to allow video display ("Ted Turner's new toy" was how the $18 million electronic innovation was characterized by local media), elected to replay a controversial call at home plate in which the Astros' Bob Watson was called safe at home after scoring on a passed ball in the fourth inning. The crowd, upon reviewing the play from a video angle that appeared to show Watson should have been called out, burst into thunderous booing.

Video review had no sanctioned role in sports officiating at this time. In fact, the umpires' basic agreement with professional baseball forbade the in-park display of controversial calls, explicitly to avoid antagonizing a crowd.

The umps in Atlanta, reacting to the kind of slap-in-the-face embarrassment that would soon become commonplace, stalked off in protest. "I knew something like this would happen," Ed Sudol, the umpiring crew chief, later explained. "Put yourself in our shoes. We could have gotten killed. It's dangerous. You get people beered up and you don't know what could happen."

The umpires remained off the field for one full minute and agreed to return to duty only upon receiving a commitment from Braves management that the scoreboard operator would, henceforth, refrain from displaying "close calls" for the amusement of the fans in attendance. (In the Big Ten, Jumbotron operators are currently urged *not* to show incendiary replays of controversial calls.)

By stomping off the field that afternoon in Atlanta, the umps were staging a kind of Luddite protest, another skirmish in the age-old clash between man and machine.

The proud men in black had drawn their line in the dirt. Getting tarred and feathered was not, from their point of view, part of their job description.

The technology, it soon became clear, was both blessing and curse. It served as a tool of immense value and an instrument of bruising humiliation.

Like any veteran ref, Hightower had his run-ins with video review. When his career began, in what seems almost like the dark ages, bitter second-guessing of officiating was pretty much limited to real-time complaints from the immediate participants and spectators, plus the media sniping that continued the following day. "We wuz robbed," that emblematic rant attributed to the manager of losing fighter Max Schmeling in the 1932 heavyweight title boxing match, summarized both the standard outrage at a bad decision by a ref and the aggrieved party's ultimate helplessness to do a darn thing about it.

Nobody likes to be robbed. And nobody likes to be accused of doing the robbing.

Video review was first introduced to college basketball in 1986, and its initial use was mainly to provide a second opinion — where was the shooter situated at the moment the shot was released? — on the far more significant innovation of that year, the introduction of the three-point line. Replay technology was also allowed for the monitoring of scoring and clock-related errors. From those early, well-defined and limited applications, video review has, blob-like, expanded at a steady clip.

"Be careful what you wish for," Gerald Boudreaux, the former

Southeastern Conference coordinator of officials, once warned about video review. "Once you open the floodgates, how much water comes through?"

Floodgates may have been a metaphor tossed off casually, yet it managed to articulate a general apprehension. The old ways of officiating had, for all the carping, served the game of basketball admirably since its invention by Dr. Naismith in 1891. True, there had been flaws. The fast-paced frenzy of ten aggressive athletes cannot be monitored with perfect accuracy by refs who cannot possibly see it all. And even if they could, the refs were bound to make mistakes. That's the way it'd always been.

The possibility that the act of officiating could be, if not actually perfected, then substantially improved by technological means was a direct challenge to the old order. Man versus machine, that hoary trope of futuristic fiction, emerged as a central tension in sports officiating. And if organized sports were forced to choose between the two, what values would inform that choice?

Each major sport has wrestled with this conundrum concerning how much to resort to technology to supplement officiating, and each sport has evolved, and is evolving, individualized solutions. Professional tennis employs the Hawk-Eye ball-tracking technology to determine whether shots are inbounds, and it is a system that has been largely accepted by players and spectators. Baseball, which had previously been permitting video review only to resolve disputes about home runs, began in the 2014 season to grant managers the right to challenge a variety of umpire calls, including trapped fly balls, tag plays, and hit by pitch. Baseball chose not, however, to allow review of strikes and balls, and there is no current plan to utilize automatic strike-zone detection, although the technology seemingly exists (witness any baseball telecast that vividly and instantly illustrates the location of a pitch superimposed on a computer-generated strike zone.) Football, particularly professional football, has developed a variety of ornate procedures for dealing with disputed calls. Each team is allowed a limited number of "challenges" covering a finite but growing list of situations (scoring plays, out-of-bounds, quarterback pass or fumble, etc.) Soccer, which places a premium on uninterrupted action, has thus far resisted mounting pressure to include video review of disputed plays. "Let it be as it is, and let's leave [football] with errors," Sepp Blatter, the president of FIFA (International Federation of Association Football), once stated.

Tennis, baseball, and football, it should be pointed out, are all sports that come with built-in pauses that naturally accommodate interludes of video review. Basketball, not so much. The aesthetic pleasures of basketball, embodied prominently in the concept of "flow," are significantly undermined when there are too many breaks in the action.

Currently, replay can be used by college basketball officials to clarify or to make determinations pertaining to errors on free throws, scoring, or time keeping; to decide whether fouls were or were not flagrant; and to ascertain during the final two minutes of a game if a shot-clock violation occurred or which player caused the ball to be deflected out-of-bounds.

Officials are allowed to check the monitor to see who should be attempting a free throw "if there is uncertainty" and replay can be used in the event of a shooting foul to determine whether two or three shots should be awarded. Similarly, with regard to scoring, officials may check replay to determine whether a made basket was a two- or three-point field goal. They may also check to rectify an error by the scorekeeper.

Video review also extends to certain matters involving timing, such as malfunctions by the shot/game clocks. These corrections are to take place "at the next dead ball" and "any activity after the mistake or malfunction has been committed and until it has been rectified shall be canceled, excluding a flagrant 1 or 2 personal foul or any technical foul."

The rules regarding replay and fouls are in flux, with alterations made almost yearly as styles of play evolve and the pressure increases to get it right. Beginning in the 2012–13 season, for example, referees were newly allowed to review any incident involving "illegal contact with an elbow above the shoulders of an opponent" to determine if a flagrant foul occurred or if officials had "plausible reason" to believe the foul was flagrant. Ever cautious about interruptions to flow, it was decreed that any review of a possible flagrant foul must take place during the next dead ball immediately following the foul.

Any ref on the court can elect to signal for video review. Coaches too can call for review in limited situations like, for example, determining if a foul was flagrant. As of this writing—an important caveat, as the improvements in technology are prompting continual reassessment of the relevant regulations—the rules regarding replay do not allow for review of "judgment calls" (traveling, for example) by the referees.

The debate surrounding video review has little to do with its efficacy. Review almost always benefits or bolsters the accuracy of a call. The problem with video review is that it takes time. It disrupts flow.

Attempts to find a middle ground are ongoing (delaying the review of a two- versus three-point field goal until the next clock stoppage, for instance), but the central conflict remains: the more frequently referees are permitted to employ video review to clarify a situation, and not incidentally insulate themselves from criticism, the more the flow of the game, and the timing of the telecast, gets disrupted. The merits of video review must therefore compete with another, often superseding agenda: moving the game along swiftly, artfully, thrillingly if possible.

It's a classic face-off. You can almost hear the hyperbolic ringside announcer introducing the combatants. In the far corner, we have Programming, wearing red, white, and blue and weighing . . . a lot. In the opposite corner, Fairness, wearing white trunks and weighing, well, maybe less than we like to think. In the middle, three guys in zebra shirts.

May the best team win.

Just how awkwardly refs can get squeezed by replay, and the restrictions on using it, was perfectly illustrated in a January 2013 clash between Kentucky and Vanderbilt. This game caused quite a stir in the officiating community. Hightower, who was not assigned to it and only learned about the brouhaha through the grapevine, immediately knew why.

Vanderbilt's Memorial Gym was built in 1952. With a seating capacity of 14,316, it is sometimes compared to Fenway Park for its peculiar configuration and the unusual complications this can cause. It's the only college basketball stadium in the country where the teams' benches are situated behind the end line, rather than the sideline. The gymnasium floor is slightly elevated, in the manner of a stage (the gym was originally built to serve many functions, not just basketball; the odd design, from the early 1950s, was not all that unusual at the time.) But the feature of Memorial Gym that had Hightower nodding in brotherly empathy concerned the placement of the shot clocks. At Vanderbilt, they are not situated above the backboard facing center court, as is customary. Instead, they are located at eye level, attached to a support pylon behind the basket and 15 feet to the right.

The Vanderbilt shot clocks were a potential problem every ref recognized. The primary purpose of having shot clocks placed prominently atop the backboard is to make the vital information they convey, those precious seconds ticking down, easily available to all the key players, and that includes the referees. The difficulties imposed by the awkward placement of the shot clocks in Memorial Gym were a disaster waiting to happen. "The farther into your periphery something gets," pointed out Dan Simons, a sports fan as well as cognitive psychologist, "the harder it is to perceive it while you're also focusing your attention on something else."

The Vanderbilt shot-clock location was like a busy traffic intersection that lacked a stoplight; an accident was bound to occur. The only question would be the degree of damage done.

"Poor officiating continues to be the story of this college basketball season," reported Deadspin the next day, "as SEC refs swallowed the whistle on a clear Kentucky shot clock violation late in the Wildcats' bout against Vanderbilt in Nashville tonight and allowed UK to march home to Lexington with a 60–58 win."

Kentucky's Nerlens Noel had hit a jumper with eighteen seconds left to put his team ahead. Replays clearly showed that the ball had not left Noel's hand when the shot clock expired.

Kentucky was then the defending national champion. Vanderbilt was, at that early phase in the season, projected as a team with "bubble" aspirations to make the NCAA tournament. A win over Kentucky would prove a very persuasive résumé item when the selection committee convened in March. And making the tournament would constitute a very meaningful accomplishment when it came time for the Vanderbilt coach to discuss contract and salary. "Every possession matters to a coach," pointed out Rich Falk, former Big Ten supervisor of officials, and former coach of Northwestern. "One bad call can make the difference in making the tournament. That's how we think."

The NCAA 2012–13 basketball rule book, specifically Rule 2, Section 13, Article 5-d, explicitly stated that officials *shall not* use available courtside replay equipment "[To] determine whether the ball was released before the sounding of the shot-clock horn," except at the very end of a game or the end of a half.

In Hightower's opinion, the referees in that Kentucky-Vanderbilt game had been hung out to dry. He was troubled less by the alleged officiating blunder — those things happen — than the media's refusal to acknowledge what he knew from firsthand experience to be an extraordinarily difficult predicament. The error the refs had made, and there was little doubt they were mistaken to have allowed Noel's basket, was almost entirely a function of being in an impossible predicament, forced to make a split-second judgment without proper access to crucial evidence.

"And," Hightower snapped with disgust at what he clearly believed was the greater indignity, "it's not even reviewable!" (Since then, the NCAA rules committee has altered its policy; now during the last two minutes of the game, officials are allowed to use the courtside monitor to determine if a shot-clock violation occurred, and also to determine which player committed a foul when there is confusion.)

Castigated by what the camera discloses yet restrained from employing it whenever needed, video review had become the quintessential rock-and-hard-place quandary. The refs, it seemed to me, were caught in the middle.

"No!" Hightower immediately corrected this observation. "We are not in the middle. We are on the outside."

. . .

On the topic of video review and its merits, Hightower related a cautionary tale — many of the anecdotes referees like to tell are essentially cautionary tales — about a game he'd worked some years back.

The date was December 22, 2004. The University of North Carolina–

Charlotte was playing at Indiana University at Bloomington, and Indiana was leading 73–71 with less than one second left. A time-out had been called by UNC–Charlotte, and they were getting ready to put the ball in play from behind their own basket. They needed to go the length of the court. The speculation in the ESPN broadcast booth was that Charlotte might, if all went very smoothly and Indiana failed to interfere, have enough time to catch a pass and give it a wild fling. "They've got to at least heave it to half court," opined the ESPN announcer during the final lull before the ball was put into play. "Probably no time for a dribble."

That's precisely what Hightower and his officiating crew were thinking as UNC prepared to make the inbounds pass.

You can look it up. Curtis Withers' inbounds pass went nearly to half-court. It was caught on the run by guard Brendan Plavich who'd been forced to backtrack in order to get open. Plavich, a 6'2" sharpshooter who once made ten three-pointers in a game against Syracuse, pivoted, took one quick dribble, then launched, with torso extended for added thrust. The long, high, seemingly slow-motion trajectory of the shot was tracked by 17,000 rowdy fans as well as the ESPN cameras that had an excellent perspective as the ball lifted in a perfect parabola before plummeting through the net.

An astounding shot; give the kid credit. But the referees had no doubt. John Higgins, the nearest ref, immediately waved it off. No basket. Time expired.

Under NCAA rules, the shot was reviewable and Hightower and his crew felt honor bound to check it out. They gathered at the scorer's table as players from both benches spilled onto the court.

"We knew the ball did not get off in time," Hightower recalled. "But I said to John [Higgins], we have to go to the monitor. We know it's not going to count, but we have to look."

With players and coaches milling about the court, Hightower and his colleagues huddled at the monitor. Viewers at home saw only their striped-shirted backs as they leaned in for a better look. Hightower, situated in the middle of the trio as the lead ref, wore headphones to communicate directly with the producer in the TV van parked just outside.

The ensuing stagecraft was familiar to casual fans and even non-fans. It's become as much an icon of American visual vocabulary as the Norman Rockwell town meetings with the gaunt Lincolnesque figure rising to speak. The three officials congregated at the video monitor atop the scorer's table. We cannot hear what they are saying to each other nor do we know precisely what details of the reviewed material are being examined. The refs hunch forward, scientists at the microscope. They point inscrutably to something on their screen. Words are exchanged. They press closer and point again. It's a kabuki ritual. We, helpless as theatergoers to affect the outcome of a gripping drama, await the verdict.

And make no mistake; these protracted interludes of video review have emerged as a feature of the sports entertainment product. The contentious second-guessing of pivotal plays supplies limitless "material" to the ranting hosts and callers of the sports talk industry. Competitive sports as an All-Dispute-All-the-Time sideshow may not be the plan, but its value is not lost on media enterprises. And its repercussions are not lost on the officials. In Bloomington that afternoon, the refs were taking longer than the fans wanted. A minute went by, then another. The TV announcers used the extra time to chew over the different video feeds they had in their possession. One wide angle from above showed the entire sequence of Plavich's final shot just as viewers saw it. An additional perspective looking directly up court from the baseline, tracking from behind the inbounds pass and the subsequent desperate half-court shot, made for thrilling viewing. In slow motion, the ball lifted from Plavich's hands, then descended as gracefully as a shuttlecock. Nothing but net.

The announcers sounded perplexed and voiced their bafflement. They too had expected confirmation that time had expired. But that's not what was revealed.

"From that angle," remarked one announcer, "it looks like there is one-tenth of a second left."

His colleague chimed in, "I can't believe Plavich got that shot off."

"Well he turned, dribbled, and shot, all in seven-tenths of a second."

As the deliberation dragged on, the mood in the arena darkened. Initially festive (*Indiana wins!*), then intrigued (*Indiana wins but it cannot be immediately verified*), it now verged on serious agitation (*seven-tenths of a frigging second; gimme a break*).

Hightower and his colleagues were completely flummoxed. "We know it's not going to count," he recalled. "We keep saying, give us another angle. And every time we run it, that ball is out of his [Plavich's] hand. Wait a minute, come on. . . . I said to John Higgins, 'We count this thing good, and we're gonna have a riot.'"

At the scorer's table, Hightower had no difficulty sensing the mounting tension. Each minute that passed by without any formal declaration that the final shot would be disallowed became the flame on a Bunsen burner, escalating the heat.

An unintended consequence of this kind of protracted confab is that the refs are suddenly catapulted onto center stage. For these fraught minutes, they are *the show*. These replay interludes become the occasion, if only because so many minutes of improvised fill-in banter are required of the announcers, to identify the refs by name. "Eddie Hightower's over there looking at *something*," reported the ESPN announcer. "Not sure what."

Interestingly, these video lulls might also present a nice opportunity, since there's time to kill, for the announcers to provide the types of amusing biographical details — hometown, personal

quirks, noteworthy accomplishments, other professional affilia-
tions! — that are the staple of sports-broadcaster filler ("favorite
snack" is one of the tidbits viewers of the Little League World
Series get to learn about the cute kids in those starting lineups).
Not so with our refs. We may have heard their names mentioned
by this point in a telecast. They may command our attention. But
their basic anonymity remains functionally preserved. They are
presented to us as generic. They wear the same uniform. They are
referees, and essentially faceless. As with the masked hangmen
of yore, whose identity had to be concealed from a potentially
vengeful community, perhaps this is best for all parties.

The Plavich shot was driving them crazy. Neither Hightower
nor his two teammates believed it was humanly possible to accomplish the several maneuvers — catching, dribbling, turning,
shooting — that Plavich had seemingly pulled off in less than one
second. But there it was on the videotape. The digital clock embedded in the lower right portion of the monitor clearly showed
0.1 at the very instant the shot was released.

So Hightower did something he'd never done before, or since.
He summoned Indiana's athletic director Rick Greenspan, who'd
been seated nearby. "I want you to see what we're seeing," he told
him. Indiana's coach, Mike Davis, sensing what might be coming,
moved to the scorer's table. The AD gestured for him to back off.

"Boy, this is going to be a tough pill to swallow," mused the ESPN
announcer. Hightower pushed back from the monitor, gave one
loud blast on his whistle, and thrust both arms decisively overhead. Basket was good.

The eruption arrived on cue. Booing cascaded from the deepest
corners. A few crumpled cardboard food trays fluttered onto the
court. The refs beat a hasty exit down the ramp beneath the stands.

Later, too late to alter the official outcome, it was discovered
that a mechanical synchronization flaw in the video feed connect-

ing the on-court cameras, the TV-production truck parked outside the arena, and the official game clock was to blame. The real-time game clock indeed had clicked down to zero. The last shot should not have counted. The refs should not have been made to appear foolish, ignoring what any fool could easily see.

Gut instinct versus objective evidence. Man versus machine. Video review giveth, and taketh away.

THE ROAD TO ASSEMBLY HALL

In Edwardsville, Hightower moves through town with the self-assurance of a man comfortably rooted in a fine and agreeable place. Impeccably attired in a swank dark suit and a lemon-lime tie, he cuts a figure of cosmopolitan elegance, pausing in the Stop'n'Save parking lot to greet a young mom who seems to know who he is, stopping by a corner table at Bella Milano's during lunch hour to chat with a trio of businessmen who'd helped in the recent campaign to finance a new high school baseball field.

Not unlike another favorite son of Illinois, he's journeyed far from his log-cabin-like origins. Several years ago, he and Barbara built a 5,500-square-foot, four-bedroom, artfully decorated Tudor house on a winding lane in an exclusive subdivision of spacious manicured lawns, and they have taken their place, unassumingly, among the community's upper echelons. He is, by most accounts, the town's MVP, and has been for several consecutive seasons. He is unquestionably its most important public official. The fact that Edwardsville is 86 percent white seemingly has no bearing on how he operates or how he is perceived.

Of course, it's not always a lovefest. In early 2011, there was some displeasure with him when a star player for the Edwardsville high school boy's basketball team, a team with high hopes of going deep into the state tournament, was kicked off for the remainder of the season. The decision to suspend the boy from the team for missing too many classes was made jointly by the coach,

the principal, and Hightower. The young man was a talented 6'3"
guard-forward with definite D-1 college potential. Appeals for re-
instatement were directed at Hightower who, it was hoped, might
see the bigger picture. And he did, although it was not the picture
that might prevail, say, at a ranking university. "It bothered me
to take the opportunity away from this young man. I understood
I wasn't doing him any favor. Athletics," Hightower added, "are a
privilege, not a right." Appeal denied.

The drive from Hightower's home to Bloomington, Indiana, should
take approximately three hours and forty-five minutes under rea-
sonable traffic and weather conditions. The route heads east on
IL-43 out of Edwardsville, past a featureless swath of modest homes
set back on multi-acre lots. Then for a few miles it joins I-55 south
toward Memphis before connecting to I-70 east for a long straight
shot. The final hour on a rural Indiana two-lane through Spencer
and Elettsville is a pastoral ride through wooded hills.

Hightower tries to make this trip in three hours and twenty
minutes. He's done it enough times to be able to clock it. Time
management is close to an obsession with him, and accelerating
his commute to games has become itself a kind of game, at which
he's been quite adept. I set off with him one bright cold Sunday
morning in late November for a scheduled 6:00 p.m. contest between Ball State and Indiana, and for once he was not rushed.

Leaving Edwardsville, we veered onto a spanking new roadway
with fresh cement curbs. It cut past a treeless subdivision reminiscent of ones carved from farmlands during the post–World War
II suburban building boom. There weren't very many homes out
this way, not yet. But that would soon change. The new road we
were traveling was an extension of Governor's Parkway, and it was
expressly fashioned to facilitate traffic to two recently constructed
public schools, Goshen Elementary and Liberty Middle School. The

perfectly rectangular lots had already been marked by ambitious developers, and would soon bloom with new home construction. "Build it and they will come," is an aphorism probably more true of the causal relationship between quality public schools and thriving communities than of fantastical baseball diamonds etched from Iowa cornfields. Which, incidentally, is precisely what this swath resembled.

"Schools are the gateway," Hightower declared proudly of Edwardsville's burgeoning prosperity. It was a statement expressing his conviction that a community's schools are its single most revealing characteristic, and that the values a community lives by are on full display in the quality of its schools. Atmospherics matter. A firm believer that first impressions are lasting impressions, he insisted that bushes, trees, and flowerbeds adorn the entranceways to each of his schools. Around each building, the playing fields, sidewalks, and parking areas were regularly groomed and kept clean. Interior corridors were buffed and shined on a daily basis. He wanted visitors to be greeted with the same style of good-natured courtesy he'd found to be reliably delivered at the Marriott hotels in which he had spent hundreds of nights. A brand that unfailingly meets consumer expectations was what he admired about Marriott's operations. His stated goal was to achieve that same brand value for Edwardsville public schools.

Purchasing the parcel on which the new schools were built and financing their construction was the result of a campaign initiated and driven by Hightower. He rallied the PTA and the business community as allies. Yet the first time the tax increase was proposed, in 1999, it was narrowly voted down. This was a bitter defeat for a superintendent determined to make public education the centerpiece of a new, forward-thinking Edwardsville. Money alone, he knew, could not buy excellence. But with it, he was certain he could work wonders.

The following year, he led a robust campaign to put the bond issue on the ballot again. This time it passed, approved by 60 percent of the voters. The town acquired the forty-eight-acre parcel of land for a price of $21,000 an acre. As of 2013, it was valued at approximately $75,000 an acre. The complex and inexact formula by which high-performing public schools translate into escalating home prices, economic development, and civic betterment might not be intricately understood by all Edwardsville residents, but it was not lost on them either.

Manny Jackson, a business-savvy former vice president of Honeywell and one of Edwardsville's most accomplished native sons, estimated that Hightower's achievements as school superintendent — the building and refurbishing of school facilities, the upgrading of the faculties and administrative staff, the influx of private donations for expanded athletic facilities, the steadily rising scores on the Illinois Standard Achievement Tests (93rd percentile for Edwardsville High, 99th percentile for Liberty Middle School in math), the introduction of state-of-the-art learning technology at all grade levels — have added as much as a billion dollars of value to the town. In 2013, Nerdwallet.com, a personal-finance website, ranked Edwardsville as the no. 1 community in Illinois for young families. "The town's public schools at every level have a near perfect rating from Great Schools," the website reported.

Jackson, one of Hightower's inner circle of local business boosters, although he now resides in Las Vegas, is a story unto himself. Raised in Edwardsville in the 1950s, he attended the all-black Lincoln School. As a young boy, he sat in the segregated balcony of the Widley Theater to watch movies, much as Hightower had to do in Hayti. The film that made the strongest impression on Jackson was *The Harlem Globetrotters*, a biopic of the heralded franchise featuring several of their gifted and flashy players. Jackson went on to become the first black to play basketball at the University of Illinois. Then he played for the Globetrotters. In 1993, he bought the Globetrotters, which he still co-owns. In 2008, he bought the Lincoln school building, scene of his own segregated education, and donated it to nearby Lewis and Clark Community College to be developed as a center for the humanities.

"Not everything that can be counted counts," Albert Einstein once famously observed, "And not everything that counts can be counted." That saying, occasionally cited by teachers displeased at being hammered by teach-to-the-test pressures, prompted a wry smile from Hightower. As much as anyone, he understood that some things can most definitely be counted, and must be. The giant scoreboard looming high above center court at game's end, for one.

The rigors of travel are the bane of referees. The majority of college basketball games are not played within major metropolitan areas that are easily reachable via direct, nonstop air travel. A change of planes is often required, along with a rental-car ride through the boonies. Moreover, in the Midwest and Northeast where Hightower predominantly works, the basketball season spans the notoriously bad weather months. It's a fortunate day when rain isn't snow, when snow is not a blizzard, when flights are landing on time despite the encroaching storm front, when the highway has been plowed and salted, when visibility extends beyond best guess.

For eighteen years, Hightower was able to neatly circumvent many of the hindrances and holdups associated with complicated air travel through a sweet arrangement with an Edwardsville-area businessman who owned several private planes. Jerry Norton, a local hardware mogul, was a basketball fan who owned twin-engine Cessna 340s as a hobby. Hightower arranged to compensate Norton the cost of fuel and pay for the copilot (Norton served as pilot), and Norton was pleased to ferry him to games for the pleasure of the experience plus a favorable insurance premium on the planes based on logging an increased amount of air miles.

At the time, Hightower was a high school principal in Alton. His schedule, as teens today might say, was crazy. With Norton as his private plane chauffeur, however, Hightower was able to work an entire school day, depart Alton High at 2:30 p.m. for the five-mile drive to Civic Memorial Field, and be in the air by 2:45 p.m. An evening weekday assignment was thus reachable at many Big Ten and Midwest campuses without cutting into his school schedule. Venues that almost always sucked up half a day or more, going and returning, were accessed by him as efficiently as if he were an eastern seaboard business commuter catching the New Haven line into Manhattan and back. Hightower could be home late the same night (very late) and sometimes repeat the process with the same schedule the very next day.

Those were the days. But fuel prices shot upward, driving the price of some routes above what he'd have to pay for commercial air. Eventually Norton's eagerness waned, favorable insurance rate or not. By 2005, Hightower reluctantly rejoined the ranks of other refs, arriving at the airport an obligatory hour-plus before departure and praying that the plane he was scheduled to take out of St. Louis wasn't stuck on the runway in Minneapolis or Denver.

Turning east onto I-70, the driving was smooth, and Hightower grew reflective. His mother was hospitalized in intensive care with a life-threatening heart condition, and just a few days before, on Thanksgiving Day, his father had died at the age of eighty-six in Hayti, Missouri. A construction worker and farmer, his father had lived his entire adult life in the same circumscribed Bootheel of southeast Missouri. Burial was scheduled for later in the week, and the anticipation of that somber occasion, plus the expectation that he would be called upon to make remarks at the funeral, had nudged Hightower's thoughts backward in time.

I would have assumed that Hightower, having been commandeered from a young age into acting as surrogate father and mentor, forsaking some measure of his own childhood in the process, would harbor some resentment toward his dad. And perhaps he did. But in his reminiscences, neither bitterness nor spite came through. Retrospect is not a perspective Hightower particularly cares to cultivate. Each game concluded is replaced by a new one looming on the schedule. "You would have liked him," he said of his father.

Hightower freely declares that he's been lucky in life. But I don't believe luck has been much of a factor, and I doubt he believes it either. The first person in his family to ever attend college, he went on to earn a doctorate in education and serve on the board of trustees of the Southern Illinois University system and Lewis and Clark Community College. Raised in a rural community too isolated and underpopulated to offer organized sports, he'd become a living emblem of just how organized sports have become. Brought up in a tin-roof shack that lacked running water, he was now owner of a sprawling two-story manse with a high-vaulted living room that looked out on a handsome fairway of a lawn and a flowering garden maintained by a professional service.

No, it hadn't been luck. Rather, his achievements were the product of a nearly letter-perfect fulfillment of every up-by-the-bootstrap, self-improvement prescription for getting ahead in the America we like to believe is the true one: hard work, perseverance, ethical behavior, determination, goal orientation, and, yes, some special talent (but not luck). The Ed Hightower story could easily be a chapter in a civics textbook.

During an extended highway lull, I asked if he ever listened to music on these long drives to basketball assignments.

Keeping his left hand firmly on the steering wheel, a fact for which I was grateful as we were speeding along over 70 mph while passing a succession of mammoth tractor-trailers, he reached with his right hand to fumble through the glove compartment.

From a plastic CD case he nimbly extracted the disc, and popped it into the dashboard sound system without comment. I tried to guess what was in store and quickly realized I hadn't a clue. His cultural tastes — favorite movies, books, music, nonathletic pastimes — had never come up in conversation.

When the Lexus audio system came on, the sound, though I had no preconceived expectations, was nonetheless a surprise: a deep sonorous male voice was speaking, not singing, with fervor.

It would probably cause concern to the profane, ill-tempered coaches whose sideline antics he'd been tasked with policing to learn that the sound-track accompaniment Ed Hightower preferred when driving long distance to their games was an assortment of fire-and-brimstone sermons. Although he also kept a handful of music CDs in the dash of his Lexus, mostly R&B from the 1960s and '70s, the recordings he most often drew on for soulful highway contemplation were religious oratory.

The fabled political speeches of Martin Luther King were represented ("The Drum Major Instinct," "I've Been to the Mountaintop," "I Have a Dream") as well as lesser-known offerings from the pulpit of Dexter Avenue Baptist like "Paul's Letter to American Christians."

But the "artist" Hightower turned to most frequently was the late Bishop Gilbert Earl (G. E.) Patterson. An iconic Memphis figure who influenced King's fateful trip to the city in April 1968 in support of the striking sanitation workers, Patterson possessed an operatic baritone that was as mesmerizing in a hushed whisper as it was in a rafter-shaking shout.

"The Compassionate Father" is where the disc was cued. Patterson's tone was rhythmic yet steady, his burning intensity only hinted at in the crisp downbeat of enunciated words. "The story is not so much about the sons, it's about the father *helping* sons. . . . It starts off talking about a lost sheep, and from there it flows to a lost coin, and finally it deals with a lost son. . . . Jesus is in the midst of *sinners*, people who really need his *help*. And the self-righteous are *condemning* Jesus because he has *time* for the sinners. . . . Jesus tells three stories and *all three* have to do with lost things."

It would not be music to everyone's ears. "It [the serenade of recorded sermons along the lonely highway heading to another basketball clash] causes me to always take inventory of myself," is how Hightower explained the appeal.

"This [basketball] is a cruel business." Hightower confided a bit later as we crossed the state line into Indiana. The eternal verities so emphatically propounded by Bishop Patterson seemed to meld with the highway's unending flatness, stirring reverie. His refereeing career was drawing to a close. There were decisions to be made about when to taper off, when to call it quits. Already he'd reduced his volume of assignments, from a high of more than seventy per season to closer to fifty. This season could, in fact, be his last.

Paradoxically, he felt that his officiating skills — his ability to run and move with dexterity, his grasp of game flow and command of the rules, his judgment under pressure and management of personnel situations — had not eroded, and were in some respects stronger than ever. Was he a step slower baseline to baseline? Probably so. But was that ameliorated by keener intuition and sharper anticipation? He had no doubt.

In the past year, Hightower had crossed that undeniable line of demarcation, the age of sixty. No longer the promising up-and-comer being nurtured and groomed for great things, he was now the stalwart veteran who had, indeed, accomplished every one of those things.

The writing was on the wall, and Dr. Hightower was nothing if not literate in the symbols by which bureaucracies communicated their intent. In 2008, he'd worked the NCAA championship game, one of the all-time classics. That overtime nail-biter between the University of Memphis, coached by John Calipari and led by freshmen prodigy Derrick Rose, and the University of Kansas of coach Bill Self and guard Mario Chalmers was replete with all the athleticism and strategy that fans of college basketball love. It was also a game widely praised for the unflappable, evenhanded performance of its officials. No bitter complaints. No cries of protest. No replays in the rearview mirror to haunt the verdict.

As the game's lead ref, Hightower stood tall. With slightly more than four minutes to play and Memphis up by five, Rose, desperate to beat the shot clock, had launched a deep, off-balance, stunningly acrobatic step-back jumper from the arc. Hightower, in the trail position, extended three fingers along his hip, the official indicator that the shot would be worth three points. When, improbably, the ball banked off the glass and went down, Hightower thrust his arms overhead, a gesture identical to the official signaling of a football touchdown. Score the bucket, three points. But running down court, Hightower was not so sure. There was an uneasiness in his gut, a disquiet he'd learned the hard way not to discount. He recalled, "I was thinking to myself, I know that I'm right [counting the shot as a three], but we've got to go take a look."

Play continued. Twenty-five seconds later, when a foul was called (on Rose, as it turned out), the resulting pause in the action presented Hightower with the opportunity. He wanted a video review, although nothing in the rulebook explicitly allowed it.

"I said [to his crew], 'Guys, we need to take a look.'"

With a live audience of 43,257 watching from their seats at San

Antonio's Alamodome and another 19.5 million TV viewers, Hightower conferred at the scorer's table with his colleagues John Cahill and Ed Corbett.

They went to the monitor, and there it was: Rose springing gymnastically backward to clear space for the shot, and the sneaker of his front foot lingering on the wrong side of the three-point arc. No doubt about it. The shot was downgraded to a two. Calipari made clear his displeasure, but you'd expect nothing less. Memphis's lead shrank by one point. Play resumed.

"You need to go on your gut," Hightower would later explain, "You need to *not* be afraid of being wrong."

Since that 2008 championship game, Hightower's number of choice assignments had, for whatever reasons, diminished. The following season, a new NCAA coordinator of officials took over. Hightower was assigned to the opening-round regional in Boise, Idaho, where he only worked the first-round game between no. 14 Cornell and no. 3 Missouri. This seeming demotion came as a surprise, and a disappointment.

In 2010, he again worked only one opening-round regional game, Old Dominion versus Notre Dame. The season after that, hampered by a shoulder injury suffered during a painful baseline collision with a power forward lunging for an errant pass, he worked only the "play-in" game to determine which of the two lowest seeds, Alabama State or Texas–San Antonio, would advance to the field of sixty-four.

Likewise, there was a drop-off in the marquee value of his Big Ten assignments. For over twenty-five years he'd been assigned to many of the notorious bitter rivalries (bitter in part because their geographic proximity often meant that some of the players on one squad had also been aggressively recruited by the opposing coach). Ohio State–Michigan State, Indiana-Purdue, Wisconsin-Illinois, were contests that, in Hightower's words, are "always, always hard, hard games." He continued to work a vigorous Big Ten schedule, but fewer of the games involved nail-biting archrival matchups, the kinds in which a desperate coach might say "he's the ref I want when we're on the road."

None of this was altogether surprising. Rick Boyages, who'd taken over as the Big Ten supervisor of officials in 2010, had made it clear that he was embarking on an initiative to repopulate and rejuvenate his platoon of referees. "We're definitely in a transition phase where the top officials over the last two decades are coming to the end of their careers," he'd stated. "We also have to bring along a new generation of officials."

Whereas Hightower may have been annoyed by this situation, he had no trouble understanding it. As superintendent of schools he had approximately 1,100 employees. As Edwardsville's buck-stops-here chief-education executive, he was constantly aware that he, more than anyone else, had responsibility for a big-picture overview of the operation and its complex objectives. The needs of the system superseded that of any individual teacher or employee. The purpose of the system was to serve the community's interest, not that of any one person. That's just the way it was, and High-tower would be the first to agree that's the way, to maximize the benefit to the largest number of people, it should be. "I do get it," he would assert with customary snap.

This season, 2012–13, he would officiate some fifty games, scattered between the Big Ten, the Big East, and the Atlantic-10 Conferences. Fifty games was a volume of assignments that would give most aspiring refs cause to rejoice. But for Hightower, it represented a step down the ladder, and retirement was increasingly on his mind. All the preconditions were in place, including perhaps the most persuasive of all, the fact the he has accomplished virtually all that he could ever have imagined or hoped for.

His only formulated goal when he first began doing intramural games at SIU-Edwardsville's Bubble Gym for $1.25 an hour, and then scrappy high school games around Alton and East St. Louis, was to make it to the college level. He had no fixed notion concerning what level of the "college level" he aspired to, or what was entailed in getting there. He did not know there was a discernible ladder ascending upward, or how this meager foothold he'd tentatively established on such a low rung might provide him a boost. He did not yet know that there were steps to take, training sessions to attend, an assortment of skills to develop and hone, canny supervisors to impress, opportunities to aggressively seize, games to play. He did not yet know, although soon enough he would learn, that he'd plunged into a competition in which a person could succeed or fail on the basis of the same attributes and disciplines that determined the fate of athletes and their teams.

He'd memorized the rule book. He'd attended rule-interpretation meetings for local refs. He's stayed in excellent physical condition. He knew what was required.

Yet he could not have imagined that this climb up the officiating ladder would eventually transport him to nearly every state in the country. He could not foretell that all the crisscrossing travel, ribbons of highway to endless skyway, would endow him with a Rand-McNally expertise in America's unsung byways. Nor could he have guessed that the far-flung hinterland trips, so beset with quirky delays and eccentric encounters, would have the unanticipated side effect of turning him into a master of the lost art of shooting the breeze with perfect strangers.

Some people respond to the nuisances of professional travel by turning inward, pulling down the cap, plugging the ear buds, hanging out the Do Not Disturb sign. Hightower, an inherently private man, would choose to go the opposite way, using each casual interaction — with the Marriott doorman who wanted to talk about last night's presidential debate, the Easton Market waitress who disclosed she'd played softball in college, the amiable retiree assisting the official scorekeeper at Ryan Arena — to wade deeper.

Now, after thirty years of touring, his arrival at college venues took on the convivial ambience of a popular congressman's return to the home district. Members of the custodial staffs clamored to say hello. Color announcers who used to be players under his jurisdiction, like Jimmy Jackson and Steve Smith, greeted him with hearty handshakes. Athletic department functionaries made a point of sharing a quip, and he had a knack for recalling enough information from their prior exchange to ask, for example, how their daughter was doing overseas in the army. Something else young Ed Hightower could not have predicted: this itinerant life of a college basketball referee would make of him a fully vested citizen of the republic, from sea to shining sea.

Exiting the interstate, we veered southeast onto Route 46 toward Bloomington. In Spencer, a pleasant town of 2,200 named after a local soldier who fought in the battle of Tippecanoe, we stopped at a McDonald's. Some referees, as scrupulous with their body's intake as any athlete, adhere to a strict health-food diet. Hightower was careful within the practical limitations imposed by getting hungry at inconvenient times in inconvenient places. Game time was approximately three hours from now. A good time to chow down, but not enough time for a sit-down meal. An occasion tailor-made for McDonald's.

The food line was unaccountably slow. The afternoon sun pouring through the picture windows onto the vanilla Formica booths lent the space the merry brightness of a day-care center. In front of us in line was a gangly ponytailed girl, a fifth grader we'd soon learn, wearing an Indiana Colts windbreaker several sizes too big. Hightower, dressed in coat and tie, was the only black man here, and the only person, man or woman, so smartly dressed. The girl stared at him with good-natured curiosity.

Hightower accepted her stare with a warm smile. "What grade are you in?"

A conversation ensued. He asked what subjects she liked, how much homework she had, what sports she played. He struck just the right tone to put her at ease, friendly and encouraging. It was the exact opposite of the snippy jock banter at which he was also adept.

She was a basketball player.

What position?

Rebounding mostly.

He asked how her team was doing.

Pretty good, mostly wins.

I was tempted to butt in and inform this lass that the man she was speaking with was a college basketball referee. Yep, that's right, I'd say. This nice man who's taking the time to ask about her life was, in fact, a famous referee who'd locked horns with no less a Hoosier personage than Bobby Knight. In a few hours' time he would be working the Indiana University game. She could watch him this very evening on TV! No kidding. For real.

But that impulse said more about me and my writer's appetites than it did about his. It conveniently imputed a prominence to Hightower and the reffing profession that hardly anyone shared, and most certainly not this guileless fifth grader. And it was most definitely not how Hightower would ever choose to introduce himself. He is a confident man with very little interest in tooting his own horn, and certainly not here, in the Spencer, Indiana, McDonald's.

Indeed, his obvious enjoyment of the interlude stemmed from the simple banality of what was being discussed. The lingua franca of elementary concerns common to school-age children and the educators who strive to reach them was the language he knew best. Besides, being a black man dressed semi-formally in a small town Midwest McDonald's on a Sunday afternoon was probably distinction enough.

Good luck, he offered when it was finally her turn at the counter to place her order.

You too, she chirped.

Bloomington, Indiana, like many Big Ten college towns, was for Hightower a veritable scrapbook of memories, not all of them entirely wonderful. The aura of Bobby Knight, gone now for more than a dozen years, still loomed large. Volatile, brilliant, autocratic, unassailable, and successful, Knight was the Hoosier men's basketball coach for twenty-nine seasons. In that time, his teams won the NCAA championship three times, the NIT championship once, and the conference championship eleven times. Most impressive, Knight managed these accomplishments without once getting slapped for recruiting violations (a subcategory of athletic programs that ought to consider forming their own conference) and maintained a commendable graduation rate for his athletes, reportedly as high as 76 percent. Knight ran a famously tight ship, strictly controlled from the top. Everyone in the program, from first-team all-Americans to lowly assistant student managers in charge of providing paper cups of water to the players during time-outs understood that they ultimately answered to Knight, and things could turn nasty if orders were not obeyed. *The Power of Negative Thinking*, was not a title he chose for his own book just to be cutesy (being cutesy was never his thing). A certain kind of glowering disgust, selectively applied, was Knight's strategic approach to achieving positive results. This tactic was not lost on referees.

Authoritarian coaches who rule like tycoons over their immediate athletic domain, as well as the adjoining academic environment in which they are ostensibly but one discrete component, was a hot topic of discussion in late 2012. A few months before, Penn State's Jerry Sandusky had been convicted of forty-five counts related to sex abuse. In July, a scathing 267-page report on the scandal, compiled by former FBI director Louis Freeh, charged that "Four of the most powerful people at the Pennsylvania State University failed to protect against a child sexual predator harming children for over a decade." The president of Penn State was named as complicit in the cover-up, along with the senior vice president for finance and the athletic director. The report was specific about where the true culpability resided, and where in the sports-dominated power structure of the university the buck ultimately stopped: longtime head football coach and venerated icon, Joe Paterno. A few weeks previously, Penn State's president, Graham Spanier, had been indicted for obstructing justice, lying under oath, and endangering children.

Nothing remotely so grotesque occurred at Indiana under the iron-fist command of Coach Knight. But the Freeh report's characterization of a campus culture that was "one of reverence" wherein "the university's athletic department was permitted to become a closed community" and was perceived by many as "an island where staff and members lived by their own rules" might easily apply to other perennially successful brand-name college sports programs, including Indiana basketball under Knight.

Were Hightower and other savvy refs aware that headstrong coaches may at times comport themselves like men who inhabit a "private island" where they're treated with "reverence" and allowed to live "by their own rules"? Did it catch their attention when a coach angrily stomping the sideline following a questionable call was received by the crowd with the adulation of Bruce Springsteen leaping onstage at the Meadowlands? Did they detect a whiff of entitlement when a head coach studiously delayed his entrance into the darkened arena in order to tease the roar of the crowd into a crescendo, and only then strutting onto the hardwood with the self-importance of a diva at La Scala?

Referees are often reminded that, save for the fact that they are singularly charged with enforcement of rules, there's a glaring imbalance of power in the arena, or at least of stature, and they just might be on the short end. Their predicament is akin to that of an itinerant circuit-court judge assigned to a rural county seat where he must face off against a popular local defense attorney, who is also the town's four-term mayor and happens to be on a first-name basis with every member of the jury plus their extended families.

Knight, Hightower emphasized, should be given credit for vigorously advocating on behalf of referees. He openly argued for greater professionalization, including upgraded pay, and lobbied the NCAA to allow referees increased opportunities for video review. In Hightower's opinion, Knight was never disdainful of the immense challenges that referees faced. He just wasn't getting paid to empathize with them, or let his empathy get in the way of victory.

Hightower was the lead ref in one the most infamous incidents involving Knight. Late in the first half of a home game in Bloomington against Illinois on February 25, 1998, Ted Valentine, a ref on Hightower's team, finally had his fill of the persistent squawking and slapped Knight with a technical. In the second half, Knight continued to harangue Valentine. When an Indiana forward lay writhing on the floor after a hard foul, Knight raced onto the court, and was eventually slapped with a second technical, and then ejected.

Hightower knew there was a history of discord between Valentine and Knight. He tried to get Valentine to rescind the second technical (it is not illegal for a coach to come onto the floor to care for an injured player). Valentine would hear nothing of it. He stood by his call.

Knight, for his part, reacted to the ejection by flinging up his arms in disgust and initially refusing to leave the court. When he did depart, it was to a rousing ovation.

No single incident got Knight fired from Indiana. Rather, it was a snowballing accumulation of reports, from players and members of the campus community, concerning various forms of intimidation, both verbal and physical. Of course there are some who hold to the view that Knight was only removed from his head coaching position once his squads ceased to dominate so consistently.

But all such speculation was background noise, nothing more than talk-show filler, gossip to enliven the sports entertainment enterprise. It is not the referees' place to question matters of university policy that take place far from the basketball court. Still, they cannot help but notice what goes on. You'd have to be blind not to.

The Ball State game was a blowout for the Hoosiers, which made it easier for me to start to implement an aspect of this project I'd hoped would prove illuminating: I wanted to learn to watch the referee instead of the ball, and try to see the game as the ref must see it.

To get there would require a level of concentration and self-denial that was anything but natural. It would be a chore. I'd need to endure a kind of deprogramming, a studied un-learning of deeply ingrained habits.

Yet I was determined to try. Pulling it off could amount to a breakthrough in perception. Like learning to love abstract art, or atonal music, or raw broccoli.

This exercise would, I hoped, be akin to foregoing sugary candies and cakes. People who've done this — not me, not yet — claim it opens up entirely new areas of taste sensitivity and allows one to savor deserts in sophisticated ways. Successfully breaking a habit for sweets depends, it's said, on finding a substitute obsession that will be just as satisfying and enriching.

A blowout — at one point Indiana went up by a score of 69–23 — provided the perfect test kitchen for this exercise. A hotly contested game between evenly matched rivals would probably have been far more diversion than I could've handled at this early stage of the practice. I watched closely as Hightower:

- Whistled a quick early foul on Ball State's very aggressive hand check far from the basket. He knew which team was heavily favored, but he was not playing favorites. And he was not about to let it get rough. Message sent.

- Hesitated a beat when a tipped ball careened out-of-bounds beneath the basket. Quickly, his eyes darted to make contact with fellow ref Mike Sanzere, situated by the three-point arc, to get a signal via facial expression if Sanzare had a better look. Sanzare indicated with a subtle shake of his head that he did not. This interaction consumed under a second. Hightower went with his gut inclination. Ball State's ball.

- Interceded when Indiana coach Tom Crean complained furiously that the Ball State player throwing the ball inbounds against Indiana's full-court press (Indiana was a whopping forty points up at the time, but refs are not paid to ask why the country's top-ranked team playing at home with a forty-point lead had chosen to clamp down with a surprise full-court press) should not have been allowed to scamper along the baseline to free himself for a better angle. The baseline was not Hightower's responsibility on the play — he was in the trail position — yet he realized Crean had a legitimate beef; the throw-in had not taken place following a bucket, in which case the scampering would have been permissible. Crean, still steaming, edged up to the ref's huddle. Hightower shooed him away. The conference lasted less than a minute; a decision was reached. Ball State would throw the ball in again, this time from a stationary position. Essentially a do-over.

- Loping easily, torso perfectly upright, head arched, trailing the flow, he assumed a position a few feet outside the three-point arc, just inside the sideline. Not much happening; Indiana worked the ball around the perimeter, zipping passes side to side in an attempt to find a seam in the energetic Ball State zone. Hightower followed the ball with unwavering attention. There was hardly a need to shuffle his feet. He could have been reclining in a lawn chair, or sipping a coke in loge 14 and not missed a thing. Then with an abruptness that could rip an Achilles tendon, he exploded in the opposite direction, knees pumping, desperately racing at full throttle to stay half a step ahead of the swift Ball State guard who'd stolen the ball and was hell-bent for the hoop.

- Hovered surprisingly close behind Indiana's Yogi Ferrell as he dribbled across half-court. Like a wildlife photographer tracking his elusive subject, he appeared certain of the right distance needed to stay close without becoming a factor.

My effort to concentrate exclusively on how Hightower performed his duties would, I recognized, be severely undermined if the game under consideration were not so lopsided, if, for example, it had been an NCAA tournament game and I was participating in the office pool and maybe a little money was involved. But still, I'd made progress. I'd convinced myself it was possible, under tightly controlled conditions, for a lifelong fan exercising an almost unprecedented level of self-control to primarily pay attention to the referee for limited stretches of time.

But could the fan go so far as to actively root for the ref?

Now *that* would be a challenge.

It was nearly 9:00 p.m. when we exited the Assembly Hall parking lot. A light drizzle, thankfully not snow, had begun to fall. Dozens of Hoosier boosters, resembling a brigade of merry Halloween pranksters in their baggy red-and-white striped pantaloons, ambled along the sidewalk.

Once we escaped greater Bloomington, the rural two-lane became very dark, even a little spooky. The sudden contrast to the buzzing, ultra-electrified megawatt frenzy of the basketball arena could not be sharper. The route back retraced the same hills of Route 46, with nothing visible except the occasional glimpse of a farmhouse with its porch light left on. It was the Sunday night of Thanksgiving weekend, and rural Indiana appeared safely tucked in. This thick blanket of tranquility did not, however, extend to Hightower's cell phone.

His brother Calvin, US Air's manager of operations at O'Hare Airport, called to go over details concerning their father's funeral, set for the end of the week back in Hayti. Their father had remarried, and there would be an additional family at the service, people who were not all that familiar to Ed and his siblings, semi-strangers who must be accorded respect. The service would be presided over by a reformed local bon vivant turned minister who'd been a great friend of Hightower's father from a long way back ("But we can't talk about *that*," the minister would eventually assure those in attendance.)

In quick succession, seemingly by prearrangement, Hightower

received calls from each of his school principals. He'd asked them to make certain their facilities were fully prepared to reopen on Monday morning after a six-day break, and to report directly to him. Accountability is paramount in a Hightower administration. For tomorrow, his primary worries were to make certain heat was functioning in all school buildings and that the plumbing had not been damaged, as the southern Illinois weather had taken a sudden dip toward freezing temperatures.

Both his daughters — Jennifer, an attorney in St. Louis who specializes in class action litigation on behalf of asbestos victims, and Julie, a Chicago-area pharmaceutical sales rep — phoned to coordinate travel plans to their grandfather's funeral and to tease their dad about various things that were lost on me. All I could hear was his deep-cackle delight at being lovingly tweaked by adoring young women.

Jennifer and Julie were, interestingly, the names of two young children whose charms had helped revive a young Ed Hightower at a low point in the early stages of his career. He'd been hired out of college to be a junior high health and phys ed teacher. But the following year, due to budget cutbacks, he'd been instead assigned to teach elementary PE. This was a significant downgrade, and he did not take it well. He complained to the Alton superintendent who said, "You will fall in love with them. Give it a try."

The superintendent was right. He did fall in love with teaching the children. He promised himself that if he ever had daughters they would be named after those four most endearing students, Lauren, Jennifer, Julie, Lynn. And so he did, and so his two daughters were named, respectively, Jennifer Lauren and Julie Lynn.

Hightower made it home from Bloomington before midnight. One of his true strengths — the kind that, like height, coaches are fond of saying simply cannot be taught — is his ability to function perfectly well on precious little sleep. Monday morning he would be in his office by 6:15 to prepare for the regular staff meeting that started promptly at 7:30.

. . .

The Edwardsville School District senior staff administrative meeting took place in a pleasant, white-walled conference room that had been annexed to the rear of the former Hadley mansion. Each of Hightower's dozen department heads took turns updating him on developments in their spheres of responsibility. The meeting moved along briskly, with reports on the acquisition of interactive whiteboards for each classroom (the result of a $1 million Hightower fund-raising initiative), preparations for holding a Grandparents Day in the elementary schools, soliciting bids from school bus companies ("I'm not interested in them telling us how great they are," Hightower cautioned his business manager, "We want them to meet *our* needs"), and plans, about which Hightower theatrically rolled his eyes, for holding the annual staff Christmas party at the Wooden Nickel Pub.

Hightower took charge of every aspect of the meeting. He was by turns genial, intense, self-effacing, demanding. His staff struck me as exceptionally bright and caring, and amusingly comfortable in how they related to him. He teased a curriculum specialist about the lack of men on her staff, and there was no lag time in her realizing it was only a tease. She quickly shot back that Hightower should give some thought to applying for a position that was coming open next month, and she promised, with a wink, to give him fair consideration. He certainly appeared to be on the receiving end of a lot of jocular affection for someone with the ironclad power to hire and fire.

Curiously, the one department report about which he seemed mildly indifferent came from Brad Bevis, the genial athletic director. Over the Thanksgiving weekend, both the boys and girls high school basketball teams had won their respective holiday tournaments, no small deal in this basketball-crazed region of Illinois. "Got to be careful," Hightower sternly warned, exaggerating his deadpan toughness to let others around the table know he was joshing, one jock to another, "about raising our community's expectations. Start winning too much and, you know, you might get fired when you finally start to lose. Been known to happen."

DISPUTED CALL IN OVERTIME

For all the persistent thanklessness that can't always be ignored, the peripatetic life of a ref can produce some pleasant surprises. There are times when it all seems to come together, and not necessarily on the basketball court.

It was a wintry Wednesday evening, Columbus, Ohio, 2011, three days after Christmas. Hightower was assigned to work the first of three contests the Big Ten network had slotted in a tight sequence during this traditionally fallow week before New Year's when there promised to be plenty of people at home with little to do. Ohio State was hosting Northwestern, starting at 4:30 p.m., followed at 7:00 p.m. by Indiana versus Michigan State, followed by Purdue at Iowa at 9:30 p.m. A college basketball fan would have no need beyond satisfying basic bodily functions to get up off the sofa until it was time for bed.

Hightower had arrived in Columbus around noon on the heels of an exceedingly hectic twenty-four hours, even by his jaded standards. The previous day at the school-district office, he'd become embroiled in a potentially nasty situation involving an Edwardsville High English teacher who was on an extended leave of absence for alleged health reasons that Hightower believed were a maneuver intended to avoid a potentially unpleasant confrontation.

Earlier in the year, the teacher had been involved in a "workplace incident," about which he declined to elaborate except to say that it did not sit well with him. Hightower had demanded the teacher meet with him, along with a union representative, as disciplinary action was looming. The teacher had avoided that meeting by taking medical leave of absence, and Hightower suspected that the teacher hoped all would be forgotten when he finally decided to return to the classroom at some future date.

All was not forgotten. Hightower was adamant that the teacher produce a credible medical report attesting to his ongoing disability. Among the thorny issues, ever present in the background, were the limited amount of discretionary spending available to find a replacement teacher, the ongoing politics of dealing with the local teachers union, and the educational needs of the students enrolled in this teacher's classes.

With the matter still simmering (the teacher would eventually be reinstated, but not until the following fall), Hightower had departed Edwardsville in the middle of that afternoon. Driving north on I-55, then east on I-72, two hours across the wintry prairie to Champaign, Illinois, he'd arrived easily in time to work the Big Ten season opener that night between Illinois and Minnesota.

The game was sloppy from the outset, an officiating challenge. Illinois seemed to have a comfortable thirteen-point lead midway through the second half, but the Gophers stormed back, and the Illini needed two free throws by center Meyers Leonard at the end to tie the game. To the delight of the fans in attendance at the former Assembly Hall, now known as State Farm Center, and those watching on TV, the game went into not one but two overtimes. For Hightower, that meant an extra ten minutes of mostly frantic game time to adjudicate, and an even later night. After showering and getting dressed (dark suit, starched shirt, tieless — even at 10:00 p.m. following two overtimes he managed to look sharp), he got back into his Lexus for the drive home. He arrived in Edwardsville shortly after midnight. Next morning, he was up before 5:00 a.m. for the drive to the St. Louis airport, where he caught a one-stop flight via Chicago to Columbus for today's late afternoon contest between Northwestern and Ohio State, one of the top-ranked teams in the country.

The byways of the cavernous Schottenstein Center, like those of most Big Ten and Big East venues, had over the years become as familiar to him as the Edwardsville School Department offices. He'd worked games at this relatively modern facility nearly two dozen times, and over the years had worked close to fifty games at Ohio State. The security procedures at big-time college sports arenas, while not as logistically daunting as one would find, say, at the Pentagon, employed some of the same measures. Hightower knew precisely which gated entrance to approach, whose name to drop in case he wasn't recognized (he was), and whom to sign in with at the sliding-glass cubicle situated just inside (everyone must sign in, although again Hightower was quickly recognized and warmly greeted by the attending clerk). Rolling his carry-on bag, he proceeded without guidance through the vast bowels of this architectural behemoth, wending his way directly to the corridor where the referees' locker room was located. There, he knew whom to ask to be let in (a combination code was required to gain access).

Another ref was already inside, naked to the waist in black biker shorts. He was seated upright on the carpet with legs extended, rubbing mentholated ointment deep into his calves while merrily whistling to himself. Eric Curry, a puckish former vice president for the Minnesota Twins, made a stage-comic display of completely ignoring Hightower, who wheeled his suitcase across the carpeted floor.

"Double overtime!" Curry shook his head in mock disgust, finally acknowledging Hightower's presence. "That is nothing but baaaad reffing."

Hightower couldn't resist a smile.

Like itinerant salesmen, referees are meticulous about the

things they must carry with them. Each ref totes his own tools, packed in modest overnighters or standard gym bags. Watching them set their bundles down before their lockers and methodically extricate the myriad contents, one by one, I was reminded of professional magicians unpacking their specialized props, without which they're sure to be exposed.

The most important thing each ref carries is his whistle, plus a back-up whistle, or two, or three. On the court, Hightower had one whistle around his neck and between his lips almost all the time, and another in his back pocket, just in case. An essential tool, *the* essential tool, the whistle is widely considered "the referee's best friend." Referees can toot theirs up to seventy-five times per game.

Modern whistles, featuring the Precision Time System, are a triumph of technological wizardry. PTS functions via a radio transmitter in the belt pack (another thing refs must be sure not to leave home without). Attached to the belt pack is an omnidirectional microphone that docks in a microphone adapter on the lanyard just below the whistle. When a ref toots, the belt pack recognizes the frequency and sends a radio signal to a receiver connected to the arena or stadium game clock, automatically stopping time.

Game shoes go in the bag. Shoes may be a ref's second-best friend. The shoes must have soles with the grip and comfort and durability of athletic shoes. They are always black, usually made of leather. Hightower spit shines his as though he were a West Point cadet facing review. He only uses a hard rubbery wax from a slender tin, no Insta Shine liquid spray for him. To preserve their shape and appearance, Hightower stuffs his with the kind of wooden shoe trees that are normally used for only the most expensive types of men's footwear.

Long black socks that stretch to the knee and provide calf muscle support, multiple pairs, go into the traveling bag. So do shoe inserts for added cushioning; black tights or compression shorts to keep the leg muscles warm and supple, black slacks sharply creased; black windbreaker-style jacket to be worn during pregame warm-ups; form-fitting, sleeveless sweat-wicking undershirts like those worn by players; long elasticized resistance bands to facilitate all manner of stretching (the host university provides the hot packs refs like pressed to their lower back during this process); and aromatic (and sometimes not so aromatic) muscle-loosening topical gels, particularly Sombra and Voltaren.

And don't forget the zebra shirt, and not just any old garment festooned with black-and-white vertical stripes. The jersey completes the uniform. It should be tapered to the torso (they like to look fit) with a thick black side panel and extra length to help keep it tucked in.

Today's Columbus contest, like the Minnesota-Illinois game Hightower had worked the night before, was the Big Ten opener for each school, the true start to the pressure-packed portion of the season. The game's third ref, Tim Clougherty, an introspective man with the no-nonsense aura of a customs agent, arrived and began unpacking. Clougherty was second-generation in this business. His father, John, was the ACC's supervisor of officials.

There was a knock at the door, and a punctilious young arena functionary poked his head in. Student interns seem to swarm around major college sports programs in hopes of wedging their foot into that gilded door. (More than three hundred universities now offer undergraduate and graduate degrees in sports business and management, providing major athletic programs with an unpaid army of eager beavers.) This young man, dressed like a teaching assistant in pale blue Oxford shirt and beige slacks, wanted merely to know if the refs needed sandwiches or anything else to eat. Orders were placed, for consumption after the game.

Each had his own routine for loosening up, a mash-up of basic health-club practices (touching toes, pulling knees tight to chest) including a variety of yoga-like stretches (on all fours, doing the cat and the camel, head arched) that targeted individual sore spots and areas of vulnerability. Hamstrings, Achilles, lower back, calves, knees, shoulders, neck, feet were all given their due. As this was taking place, Hightower led a discussion about "points of emphasis" that, from time to time, the NCAA and the Big Ten choose to flag for the officials. Hand checking and rough play in the paint were currently on the docket. The flow of the conversation was not unlike what a sales team might engage in prior to pitching a big account, working off a familiar checklist in preparation for closing the deal.

Hightower pointed out that Northwestern would probably try to slow the pace, given Ohio State's offensive superiority; no more needed to be said about the surveillance demands that would place on their officiating duties. The Ohio State guard, Hightower warned, had exceptionally sneaky hands, often went for the steal at unexpected times, and often succeeded. Make sure you really see a foul, *really* see it, before calling it. All nod.

The game proved relatively easy, both for the crew of referees and for the host Buckeyes. Ohio State took the lead early and it was never really close. Their smothering defense held the Wildcats' top scorers, senior John Surna and junior Drew Crawford, to thirteen points below their combined average. There was some intermittent yelping from the benches, but it lacked conviction and seemed mostly meant to showcase the fact that the coaches and their assistants were paying attention. At one point in the second half, as Ohio State prepared to put the ball into play following a time-out, Buckeye coach Thad Matta sidled up to Clougherty for a quick, furtive conference. Afterward, I asked what had been said. "He told me to get ready to blow my whistle," Clougherty chuckled, "because he'd designed a play that was going straight into Sullinger and he said there was no way Northwestern could stop it without fouling."

Final score, 87–54, Buckeyes. A game that had not been entirely grueling from start to finish was perfectly fine by the refs. And especially welcome this afternoon for Hightower.

Immediately after the game, Curry hit the road. He had a four-hour drive still ahead of him tonight, up to Ann Arbor, where he would work an afternoon contest tomorrow. Hightower and Clougherty returned to the Columbus Airport Marriott and went straight for the restaurant, just off the lobby. Hightower needed to be on a 6:30 a.m. flight back the next morning, but had just enough time for a leisurely meal ("modern American classic" was the River City Grille's cuisine specialty) and just enough energy to possibly enjoy it.

No sooner had Clougherty and Hightower ordered (salad and enchilada, respectively), then they glanced up at a handsome African-American man in a tight-fitting pullover shirt and designer jeans who'd just entered. They seemed to recognize him. The man looked familiar to me also. From where? Possibly TV sports?

Surveying the River City Grille for a place to sit (near the big TV or far from it?), the man spotted Hightower and Clougherty. Immediately, they waved him over and were on their feet, handshakes extended, by the time he arrived.

Danny Crawford was a much-respected NBA ref (he would be the lead ref in the 2013 Heat versus Spurs seventh game) and on being introduced I realized he was familiar and not just from TV viewings. He was the man I'd encountered several years back on that Chicago-bound flight, the one whose dogged scrutinizing of a jump-ball breakaway sequence on a laptop video had so intrigued me.

Crawford had flown to Columbus from Miami, where the previous night he'd officiated the Heat versus Celtics game on national TV. Crawford's son, Drew, was the shooting guard for Northwestern. Given the demands of his own arduous schedule (NBA refs work seventy to eighty games and are required to arrive in the host city the day *before* each game), this was a relatively rare chance for Crawford to see his son play. Since the game ended early in the evening, he'd hoped for a visit with his son and to possibly catch a meal together (the Wildcats would be staying in Columbus overnight). But the OSU game had put Drew in a sullen mood. He was angry at himself for the way he and his teammates had played, and had decided this was not the evening to hang out with dad.

Crawford explained this to Hightower and Clougherty with a shrug of regret, but he allowed that Drew's irritability after a poor performance was hopefully an indicator of strength of character. The good ones are like that, Crawford noted, grudgingly making his peace with the situation.

The Gay '90s (1890s) was the interior design motif behind River City Grille. The three refs sat beneath an imitation gas lantern by the frosted-glass space divider. Other than the bartender and the giant TV, they had this wood-paneled alcove all to themselves. Crawford and Clougherty ordered up beers. Hightower abstained. The service was not the swiftest. There was plenty of time to talk, and no lack of topics. Amiably, they swapped stories, members of the same tribe, united by a common language and a shared set of experiences. Crawford treated the college refs to an anecdote about LeBron, and they all agreed there was no NBA equivalent of officiating a Duke home game with Coach K orchestrating the crowd like they were the marching band and he was the conductor. Star players like LeBron and Kobe were the focal point of the pro game. In college, it was clearly the coaches.

To the casual fan — OK, the casual fan touched with a bit of cynicism — prominent D-1 coaches with their multimillion dollar contracts and outside endorsement deals can appear to be the root of what ails college sports, or at least the symbol of it. I'd tried several times to prod Hightower into disclosing what I felt certain had to be his private reservations about hard-driving coaches and their Fortune 500 programs. I'd overheard other refs giving voice, off the record, to observations that were distinctly unflattering. In a conversation about why Tubby Smith had been fired as coach from the University of Kentucky, one ref told me, "They replaced him with a cheater who couldn't win. And they replaced *him* with a cheater who *could*." But Hightower would go no further in his criticism than to say, "It's an extremely difficult job and I wouldn't want it for the world."

I'm not exactly sure how the pea-less whistle popped into the discussion but I think it was in response to a question I'd raised about whether any referees had gone on to notable accomplishments outside of sports. I understood, of course, that a profession that places a premium on cultivating a quasi invisibility, interrupted only by episodes of high-profile scorn and derision, might not be an ideal launching pad to prominence in other walks of life.

The first name to pop up was Irv Brown. A former college basketball ref who worked six Final Fours, including those dominated by Lew Alcindor and Bill Walton, Brown went on to become a popular sports talk show host in Denver. Hightower, Clougherty, and Crawford all knew of Brown. But they had to scratch their heads a minute to come up with another brother ref who'd managed to achieve renown. Then it came to all three of them, almost simultaneously: Foxcroft, Ron. The Fox 40. The pea-less whistle!

It's easier to officiate a contest hobbling on crutches with two broken ankles than to do so without a trustworthy whistle. The pea whistle is the type familiar to most of us. Made of plastic or metal, pea whistles rely on a small cork ball in the whistle's chamber to create a trilling, vibrato effect that serves to distinguish and intensify the sound. The strangely named Acme Thunderer, developed in England in the 1870s, was the most popular of such models.

The pea, as it turned out, was less than completely reliable. Several conditions jeopardized its fidelity, from saliva buildup in the chamber to stickiness on the surface of the pea caused by food particles or beverage ingredients swimming around in saliva. Fastidious refs avoided sugary soft drinks before and during games. Ultrafastidious refs boiled their whistle before each game. Worst-case fear was that the whistle might jam, stifling all sound. A referee forced to make a crucial call with a muted, malfunctioning whistle is like a . . . well, feel free to create your own analogy, so long as the punch line concludes in frustration, embarrassment, impotence, and dereliction of duty. That is exactly what Ron Foxcroft experienced while officiating at the 1976 Montreal Olympics.

During the gold-medal game between the United States and Yugoslavia, Foxcroft witnessed an obvious elbowing foul by a Yugoslav player but lacked the tool to stop play. He puffed and he puffed and he . . . but no sound emerged. A moment later, Foxcroft found himself being pummeled with catcalls from a packed stadium of 18,000 agitated pro-American fans. From that humiliation was born the idea for the Fox 40 Classic Pealess.

This whistle creates a piercing, stop-action screech purely by air-pressure mechanics. It reputedly emits a sound shriller and more penetrating than that of the pea whistle. It is the gold-standard whistle today for sports officials, even more so owing to the technological adaptations that allow it to be synched with the scorer's clock. Like the contractor's measuring tape or the jeweler's loupe, the whistle is a tool that may seem pedestrian to the lay observer but is prized by the craftsman who must depend on it. Foxcroft takes pride in promoting his whistle "like it was a precision medical instrument."

The River City Grille's flat-screen TV was situated high above the bar, beside a dark wood bookshelf meant to appear homey with its

Funk & Wagnalls encyclopedia collection and bound volumes of Readers Digest Condensed Books. A college basketball game was in progress. The audio was turned demurely low, and presented no intrusion as the conversation veered from pea-less whistles to updates about mutual friends back in Illinois (Crawford is a Chicagoan) to Clougherty's brief flirtation with becoming a baseball umpire. I'd expected that these refs' full immersion in sports must eventually reach a saturation point and, unlike a lot of fans who can never get enough, these guys probably sometimes could. Road-weary veterans who find themselves, whether at the end of the season or the end of a long string of games, or simply at the end of a very long day like this, sated with the sport of basketball would be oddly endearing. Lifeguards, allegedly, don't make a habit of going to the beach on their days off.

I took this occasion to query Crawford, the NBA pro, on my pet theory that officiating, viewed a certain way, provides an illuminating glimpse into the complexities of our system of justice. This notion, half-baked and decidedly arguable, was one that I'd grown rather fond of. Quickly, I realized Crawford was not even listening to me. Something in the basketball game on the TV above the bar had caught his eye. Apparently he *had* been slyly glancing that way. And so, apparently, had the other two.

It was Indiana versus Michigan State, the middle of the three Big Ten Network telecasts this evening. A blocking foul had been called on Indiana's Cody Zeller. Crawford shook his head; he was not so sure the call was correct. Clougherty felt it was. Hightower also had been watching and he too had his doubts. By God, they did watch the sport during downtime of their civilian life! But they sure didn't watch it the way a fan would. Valentine, Mike Kitts, and Ray Perone were the refs working this game. Did they have the best sight line for the calls they made? Was this recent call consistent with another down low, when Zeller was on offense pushing for position? Their eagerness to second-guess the ref's decision was typical of any myopic fan. But the underlying nuances in their reasons for doing so were strictly a connoisseur's.

Indiana, losing ground, called time-out. Crawford's attention returned to our conversation, although he proved less than smitten with my philosophical musings. No problem. Being disputed beats being ignored, and I was about to slide into another pet conjecture when I noticed Crawford's gaze had drifted again to the TV.

We were seated fifteen feet from the screen. The players, miniaturized from this vantage point, appeared as toy soldiers zipping across an imitation battlefield. Indiana's Jordan Hulls, trying to slow a cut into the lane by MSU's Keith Appling, was called for a foul. An unremarkable garden-variety infraction, unworthy of any fan's attention, yet each ref surprisingly had an opinion — was it a foul, should it have been called, was it consistent with an earlier non-call that had been completely overlooked by me, but not by them?

Meals were served. The next forty-five minutes passed with a mix of shoptalk, intermittent eyeing of the TV, and pleasant food and drink. And yes, like any group of ill-informed guys in any tavern in any town in America, the banter included praising a remarkable no-look pass, saluting a high-flying dunk, and second-guessing the ref. I'd thought referees were different from you and me. And they are. Yet off duty, they are liable to lapse into acting like plain folk, which is to say fans.

The evening dragged on. The Indiana–Michigan State game wound down, and the Purdue-Iowa game promptly took its place on the screen. Time to head upstairs, flop onto the comfortable Marriott king size, and catch some sleep before the wake-up call. Handshakes all around were cordially exchanged.

At the final good-bye, Crawford edged closer. His joviality slipped away and he fixed Hightower with a look that verged on a scowl. He had a bone to pick. They were standing toe to toe, in the quiet yellow glow of the River City Grille's faux gas lamp, beside the frosted-glass space divider.

"That call you made on Drew?"

Hightower nodded. He remembered the call. He seemingly remembered all the calls he makes in the course of a game, a fact I found truly astonishing since they come so fast and furious, and the cumulative action of each game seemed to me like an ocean wave crashing ashore, its turbulence transforming all that came before into undifferentiated grains of sand. Not to Hightower. He looked hard at Crawford. He knew exactly which whistle was being called into question. It was Drew's second foul, nine minutes into the first half. It put Drew on the bench for a long stretch, effectively constraining his play for the remainder of the half, and crimping what little flow Northwestern imagined itself to be mustering (and not incidentally cutting into the precious time Danny had to watch his son play.)

"You got that one wrong," Crawford insisted.

Hightower smiled, but it was patently insincere, absent of good will.

"Drew had position."

"Not at the point of contact."

"Well, my friend, I disagree."

"That's your right, Danny." Hightower said this with a firm, measured, dispassionate tone he often employs when assuring irate coaches that their complaint will be heard so long as it stays within the bounds of civility and does not threaten to become a sideshow. "But the call was correct."

Crawford stepped back to clear a little space. He wanted to demonstrate what he believed occurred—what occurred some four hours ago, under the blazing bright lights of the 16,000-seat Schottenstein Center, at the end of the court nearest the Ohio

State band, on the right side of the lane as you faced the basket, with Deshaun Thomas coming off a pick by Jared Sullinger and . . .

Hightower had heard enough. He did not need or want a reenactment. With a deep-chested musical chuckle, at once cheerful and dismissive, he let Crawford know that the conversation had exhausted its allotted time. He could have been addressing John Calipari at the scorer's table or the aggrieved parent of a truant sophomore.

"Agree to disagree," Hightower said jovially, and conclusively. "That one, Ed, you got wrong."

They did shake hands, amicably yet stiffly, and Crawford headed for the lobby.

"That," Hightower explained, in effect summing up so many of the thorny dilemmas he adeptly negotiates, "was a father talking. *Not* a referee."

ROOTING FOR THE REF

Could I train myself to watch a game of basketball by following the ref? Could I succeed in tracking the action through a lens other than the one I'd spent my entire sports-fan career peering through? Could a game be enjoyed in this way?

It had helped to focus on a single referee, one whose experiences could illuminate and guide me, one whose perspective I could try to share. Now Ed Hightower, after nearly thirty years, was set to retire from the game. What could be learned from that?

He'd decided against working one last NCAA tournament. It had been several years since his last finals, the Memphis versus Kansas overtime classic, and he sensed that he wasn't likely to get another crack at the Big One. It happens, to players, to coaches, and, yes, to referees. New talent is always surging forth and sooner or later it will have its day. That's usually the case with sports and other highly competitive spheres of activity. It might not always be precisely fair, but who's to say?

The 2013 season's-end Big Ten championship tournament would be Hightower's last. The Big Ten was the conference where he'd officiated the most games. He'd worked its annual tourney every year since its inception. In fact, he'd been on the floor for every single Big Ten championship final game until three years ago when he was on the DL with an injured shoulder. If it could ever be said of any referee that he occupies something akin to a home field, a place where he is known to the crowd and intimate with the setting, it would have to be Hightower at the Big Ten tournament. It had been the scene of many memorable games and the long list of all-American players whom he'd whistled, rebuked, encouraged, warned, chastened, and affectionately chided over the years included Deron Williams, Mike Conley, Devin Harris, Jimmy Jackson, Glen Rice, Calbert Cheaney, Zach Randolph, Evan Turner, Chris Webber, Jared Sullinger, Jalen Rose, Glen Robinson, and more.

Hightower's affiliation with the conference had begun in humbler times, for him and for the league. Today, the Big Ten, as much as any college conference, stands as a showcase for the grand extravaganza of college sports in America. Financially, it is the most successful, partly due to the extremely profitable Big Ten Network, which the league owns jointly with Fox. In 2012, six Big Ten schools were among the top twenty in the nation in athletic revenues, and all eleven programs ranked in the top thirty-five. Big Ten commissioner Jim Delaney received $2.8 million in compensation in 2012, and the top basketball coaches were paid between $2 million and $4 million annually. Even a coach with a lower-tier salary like Iowa's Fran MacCaffrey ($1.61 million) had a contract with substantial bonus incentives for reaching the NCAA tournament ($200,000), for each tournament win ($50,000) and for reaching the Final Four ($100,000).

Chicago was the site of the 2013 Big Ten tournament, and the 20,000-seat United Center, wedged uncomfortably into a high-crime West Side neighborhood, would be the upscale scene of Hightower's swan song.

The Big Ten championship, scheduled every year during the week prior to the start of the NCAA tournament, was a single-elimination tourney that consisted of a nearly twelve-hour slate of games throughout its opening day, always a Thursday, followed by a reduced schedule on the ensuing days leading to the championship game on Sunday. The winner received the conference's automatic bid to the NCAA tournament.

Hightower knew in advance that he would work the two opening rounds, Thursday and Friday. What he did not know in advance, nor did any of the refs, was which game he would be assigned, or at what time of the day or evening. For some undeclared reason that seemed to befuddle many of the refs, the Big Ten elects to withhold notification of the next day's ref assignments until late on the night before.

There's no question that a control-freak mentality permeates the management of the conference. This impulse, I should add, is no different than what you would expect to encounter at any large company with diversified holdings, a sizable workforce spread across many satellite offices, numerous stakeholders with divergent agendas, and a valuable brand that needs to be constantly tweaked and polished.

That the Big Ten is big business comes as no surprise (same with NCAA football, and the March Madness spectacle). The conference boasts a megabucks TV contract, its very own TV network, colossal basketball arenas and football stadiums, a bevy of corporate "partners" that includes BMW, Allstate, Verizon, and Nike, a paid-subscription digital network, and a 50,000-square-foot office building planned for suburban Rosemont, Illinois, near O'Hare Airport, that will house an interactive museum extolling the grand history of "The Big Ten Experience." The banner of prosperity is proudly raised high.

For the 2013 tournament, the Big Ten had set up its command center at the elegant Four Seasons hotel just off Michigan Avenue. Over the course of four days, university administrators and trustees, alumni and well-heeled boosters, athletic-department personnel and conference officials would gather in the swank lobby with its muted light and plush sofas for a moveable feast of sports administration shoptalk.

What Cannes is for the movie industry, this annual get-together seemed to be for Big Ten athletic community. The opulent Four Seasons' lobby functioned as an exclusive watering hole in which to strut and schmooze and celebrate the industry. Look, there goes Michigan State's Tom Izzo. Look, there's ESPN's Gus Johnson. Look, isn't that . . . Ed Hightower?

The refs also stayed at the Four Seasons, and it was a nice touch, bringing them into the luxurious tent. Not nearly as prominent as the head coaches (directors) yet better known than many of the players (lead actors), and certainly more recognizable than the university honchos and boosters (producers), the refs appeared in the indispensable role of character actors, familiar faces delivering reliable high-quality performances regardless of the script. Look, isn't that Ted Valentine?

The Friday night second-round contest between Ohio State and Nebraska, a surprise winner over Purdue the night before, would be Hightower's final Big Ten game. He'd learned already that he wasn't selected to work the finals. Thirty-some years earlier he'd trotted onto the bright lights of this big stage utterly unannounced, and that was how he would depart, without fanfare. A whimper not a bang. Perfectly fitting, come to think of it.

What would also be fitting, it occurred to me, would be to have it all culminate in one last gutsy, game-deciding, coach-provoking, crowd-infuriating, *SportsCenter* display of grace under fire, a brave flashing of zebra-stripe and shrieking whistle that boldly resolved the conflict, fair and square. What I envisioned was the kind of dramatic call that would amount to the referee equivalent of a walk-off home run (if you'll permit me a mixed sports analogy this late in the game).

I'd been reluctant to admit to Hightower that my mind veered in such hackneyed directions. Throughout our conversations, he'd tried to get me to dial down this impulse to dramatize what it is that he and his referee colleagues do on the court. Still, I couldn't abandon the notion that it would be a most appropriate capstone if this one ended, say, on the very last play with Hightower hunkered at the baseline, whistle fixed in puffed cheeks, face to face with a goaltending dilemma or a block/charge with bodies flying or a brutal back screen that'd miraculously parted the lane like the Red Sea. It would be a call that no mere mortal could make, a situation outside the purview of video review, a dire dispute that could only be settled, as settled it must be, by the lone sheriff, standing fearless and tall. It would be a call to send the astonished fans home breathless and fuming, with jangled nerves and a pounding in their ears.

How the heck did he do it? How did he pull it off? Ah, only the great ones can.

In the final interlude before the Nebraska–Ohio State game began, Hightower went through a small series of gestures and gyrations that had become a kind of ritual. He stood at mid-court with his back to the scorer's table. He bent at the waist for a final limbering of lower back and hamstrings. He was no longer the lean and hungry welterweight of decades past. A bit fleshier across the midsection, and rounder in the cheeks and chin, a happier face by and large. Gazing at the teams wrapping up their shootaround, he stretched side to side, swiveling his shoulders. The Nebraska band, mostly tubas, trumpets, and trombones — a skeleton crew compared to the grand ensemble that performs at football halftime in Lincoln, launched into a pop tune by the Fleet Foxes. I doubt Hightower knew the song. Yet there's a sameness to college marching-band arrangements, no matter the melody, and Hightower started to sway ever so slightly.

Big Ten Network announcer Gus Johnson strolled by and

they exchanged quick pleasantries. A silver-haired man in a navy suit — an announcer? an Allstate executive? — greeted Hightower with a hearty handshake. An overweight bald guy with glasses, not a typical look at courtside, approached. A TV statistician? A frowzy newspaper reporter? Soon they were both laughing. A bearded man in jeans with an impressive array of elongated camera lenses around his neck sauntered over. Hearty handshakes again.

Aaron Craft, the Buckeye point guard, drifted over from the layup line to say hello. This was Craft's junior year and by now Hightower had refereed nearly a dozen of his games. (I'd once asked Dr. Lynda Andre, Edwardsville's assistant superintendent for curriculum and instruction, if Hightower's basketball prominence affected how he was perceived by students in the district. "Sometimes he'll make a classroom visit," she told me, "and they'll get excited and want to know, 'Like, do you really know Jared Sullinger? Do you really know Aaron Craft?'") For the record, Craft was a premed major with a 3.9 grade point average, a living billboard for the vanishing breed of student athlete.

This steady parade of well-wishers suggested a carefully orchestrated farewell party (neither of his ref colleagues for this game, both well-respected veterans, experienced anything similar) but he'd made no such announcement. The truth is, this was typical of the flow surrounding him in the final interlude before tip-off of nearly every game he worked. The bands are playing, players are finishing their warm-ups, and the people employed in operations, TV producers and technicians, security guards, scorekeepers, arena personnel, drift aimlessly about, coolly taking five before the action erupts. Over the course of countless games, they'd become Hightower's people. He'd taken the time to pay them respect like a skilled retail politician, and the cordiality had been returned. They may not know much about him. But they were pretty sure he was not the "Worst F**king Ref in the world."

As the starting lineups were introduced, he stood placidly between his two referee partners. Solemnly, they knocked fists, a starting lineup unto themselves, determined to go out there and play their best.

The Ohio State and Nebraska players had already arranged themselves around the center circle when Hightower stepped between them, holding the ball at his chest. A quick glance around the circumference told him that all the contestants were at the starting line, raring to go.

He was the only person among those gathered at center court that did not appear pumped up, at least not visibly. His colleagues had taken up positions deeper into their respective backcourts. The two tall centers dipped their knees for added spring, and readied their half-raised inside arms. Once he was satisfied that all was well, that the players had finalized their positions around the circle, Hightower wasted no time. With a deft two-hand underhand flip, nonchalant as a shrug, he hoisted the ball upward. As the two centers leapt to swat at the ball, he held his ground for safety's sake, the sole stationary figure in this suddenly animated tableaux. Play ball.

Did he pause to reflect, as the tossup was swatted into play, on the implications of this being his final Big Ten game? If so, this would be the juncture, deftly filtered through Hightower's imagined thought process, for a neat capsule recounting of his career and the emotions sweeping over him as it drew to a close. Not going to happen. Once the game starts it will consume 100 percent of his attention. Indeed, the full mental immersion demanded of basketball officiating is, for many refs, a welcome psychological benefit. All worldly concerns are subsumed by this urgent call to duty. Absorption in the game becomes a kind of reprieve from other concerns, an excuse to think of nothing else, almost like a vacation except for the fact that there's nothing peaceful, leisurely, or stress-free about it.

Three minutes in, Hightower whistled a Nebraska guard for a hand check near half-court. A bearded man seated almost directly in front of me, who I'd only noticed because his companion resembled the gruff New England Patriots coach Bill Belichick but probably wasn't, erupted, "Come on, Hightower. Let 'em play!"

It was not a shooting foul and as Ohio State put the ball back in play, I tapped the complainer on the shoulder to ask a pressing question. The night before, at Hightower's opening-round game between Purdue and Nebraska, the exact same thing had occurred. Several minutes in, Hightower had called a reaching-in foul on Purdue. From across the stadium (the United Center was downright quiet compared to raucous campus arenas packed with noisy home-team partisans), a perturbed male voice had belted out, "Let 'em play, Hightower!"

The bearded fellow beside the Belichick imposter turned to face me. I saw that the forest green sweatshirt he was wearing was labeled "Spartans." Michigan State was slotted for the evening's next game. This fellow was not even a fan of either team now playing. Why, I wondered, was he so worked up?

"Out of curiosity," I asked him, "did you yell out the same thing last night? About Hightower?"

"No. I wasn't here last night."

"That's odd." And I told him why I'd asked.

"Oh, everyone says that," he assured me with no obvious rancor. "He's the only ref we know by name."

Stationed behind the baseline, Hightower shuffled a few feet this way and that, as Ohio State whipped the ball around the periphery of the three-point arc, seeking a seam in the Nebraska zone. A pass was slapped away and Nebraska grabbed it. Instantly, both teams bolted to the opposite end. From a languid lateral shuffle, Hightower was forced to accelerate into an all-out sprint, an impressive zero-to-sixty undertaking, in automotive parlance. He dipped his torso for added thrust while keeping his head vertical, eyes wide, whistle tight between lips, cheeks puffing. Now in the trail position, he couldn't afford to lag. Racing, he kept furtively glancing around, like an escapee fleeing the cops, to make certain the fleet Nebraska attack, time's wingèd chariot personified, was not pulling away.

Under my breath, or possibly not, I cheered him on: Go, Ed, go! Amazingly, he pulled it off, staying just a few measured strides nearby as the sleek young athlete shot toward the basket. Yes!

I realized I'd grown as familiar with Hightower's moves as those of any player I'd ever watched as a fan: his style of running with torso upright atop motoring legs; how he tucks his elbows and with a pronounced sideways heave, almost a chorus-line gesture, briskly reverses direction; the mask of inscrutability he wears beneath the hoop as he surveys his domain like a ship's captain in dangerous waters. These moves, similar in this respect to Kobe Bryant's fade-away jumper or Dustin Pedroia's batting stance, were thoroughly generic yet highly personalized, a signature way of maneuvering through space to achieve the desired goal.

He's as edgy as a cat burglar, never still. Tonight was no different. Watching him, whistle jutting from lips, eyes beaded in constant surveillance, quick feet alert for the starter's gun, on the prowl, prepared to flee, ever vigilant, it occurred to me that only a head coach afraid for his job would bother scrutinizing each microsecond of the game with such relentless intensity. Hightower combined an elite athlete's sixth sense with a shrewd street cop's nose for trouble brewing. Many major sports — baseball and tennis, most prominently — tout hand-eye coordination as the single most indispensable ingredient for success. With refs, the crucial asset might be something like eye–mind's eye coordination.

There was a timeout. Hightower stood courtside, holding the game ball, staring abstractly at the cavorting OSU cheerleaders, who certainly had their work cut out for them trying to animate this less-than-capacity crowd, only a small portion of which were here to watch the Buckeyes. Coming out of the timeout, Deshaun Thomas, Ohio's leading scorer, approached Hightower for a brief exchange that ended with a big smile on both. This casual fraternizing with players, sometimes taking them aside and throwing his arm over their shoulder like a school principal, or truant officer, or compassionate father, for a private scolding was one of the characteristic moves that his detractors most detested about Hightower; to them, be they fans of the Badgers, the Boilermakers, the Hawkeyes, the Hoyas, the Illini, the Wolverines, the Owls or Cardinals or Spartans or Wildcats or Bearcats, Hightower's chumminess toward the players bespoke a host of hidden biases and possibly the more deplorable lust to seek kinship with the athletes, to view himself on a par with them, to elevate, as it were, beyond his station.

The truth, of course, was probably even more subversive. The athletes were young men who can never get too much guidance or too much support from trustworthy authority figures. Hightower the referee perfectly understood there was no room for sociological distinctions once the game began. But Hightower the educator had a viewpoint that was never entirely absent.

Behind the baseline, a wide body was blocking his angle. Hightower leaned his entire torso sideways, like a cartoon snoop peering around a corner. The ball swung the other way. Hurriedly, he shuffled for a better look. Contact on the shot, but no call. The Nebraska coach, screaming, disagreed, not so respectfully.

Now at the other end, he was working the center position of the ever-shifting triangle, stationed at the sideline parallel to the free-throw line. A deflected pass hurtled back toward half-court, was promptly retrieved, and swiftly rifled back into the paint. Sensing that the lead ref could use some help, he hustled nearer, utilizing a highly efficient side-skip straight out of gym class, one leg shooting out laterally, the other snapping ahead to meet it. And sure enough, proving the effort was not for naught, he arrived as Johnny-on-the-spot at the ideal coordinates of time and space to witness Deshaun Thomas getting nicked on the forearm while in the act of shooting. It was a foul that might easily have escaped notice by the other two refs, given their locations elsewhere on the floor. But it would certainly *not* have escaped notice by the Buckeye bench or the Big Ten network announcing crew. Score another for Hightower!

And it was at this moment that I realized: I'd actually done it! This enthralling invention of Dr. Naismith's, this jigsaw amalgam of passing and shooting and picking and defending and rebounding and rolling had, finally, been transmuted into a shadow refraction of this brand new, hard-earned, alternative focus. The gyrations of the bouncing ball and the extravaganza of artful offensive theatrics were still present, of course. But the depth-of-field emphasis that once dominated my basketball viewing had, through a refocusing of the binoculars, gone fuzzy and indistinct. The ball was now the backdrop. My field glasses were trained on the sharper image, suddenly in the foreground, of the invisible gorilla. A good man in a zebra shirt was working hard at a tough job, and it was something to behold.

Getting to this stage of discernment had exacted a price. It had required self-discipline and a bit of self-denial. But is that not always the case with pursuits that force us beyond the comfort zone?

I'd done it! I was watching the ref!

I was watching as Hightower flew like a wide receiver tight to the sideline, then abruptly curled just in the nick of time to witness the defender's sly (clean!) strip of the ball. I was watching as he enacted a sweet matador swivel to avoid being slammed by a raging forward lunging desperately for a loose ball (failure to avoid exactly this type of collision cost him a portion of the 2010 season with a shoulder injury) while simultaneously craning his neck to monitor what damage the unbalanced bull was going to cause next. I was watching him as he prowled the trail position, a tiger eyeing its prey, blended into the environment, unnoticed.

As Nebraska worked the ball perfunctorily from side to side, getting nowhere, he tracked the plodding, repetitive back-and-forth passes. Motionless except for the darting of his eyes, he was like a World Cup soccer goalie who can do nothing except stay vigilant as the real action takes place far downfield. He is as useless a spectator in the upper balcony until . . . until . . . until the action shifts and his services are suddenly, desperately needed.

Several minutes into the second half of the Nebraska–Ohio State game, it was officially a blowout. OSU has stretched its lead to twenty-two points. It was clear by now that Hightower's career as a Big Ten referee was not going to have a storybook finish. It was not going down to the wire. No fateful, gutsy, last second, outcome-deciding call was going to be available to him. There would be no brave refusal on the game's final possession to fall for the up-fake that sends the defender toppling deviously backward like an axed tree. There would be no final caucus at the scorer's table after time's expired, isolated from the clamor by bulging earmuff headphones.

No, this one would end without fanfare. Or at least without the kind of fanfare we fans most enjoy snacking on. Too bad? Well, that depends on what we'd come here to see.

Me, I'd come tonight to root for the ref. Not just *watch* the ref, mind you. Not just admire him as an actor on a stage, though he was certainly that. Not just study his footwork and positioning. Not just log and evaluate each decision, tipping a hat each time he swished one from the corner.

No, what I'd come to do was *root* for the ref. As would a fan. I wanted him to play well. I wanted him to shine. I wanted him to win. And his victory did not have to wait until the very last seconds of the game.

With 7:58 to play, there was a time-out. Hightower stood at parade rest across from the benches, holding the game ball, eyes sweeping the upper reaches of the United Center seating. A trio of Ohio State cheerleaders tumbled by, and the OSU band broke into a brassy rendition of "Hang On, Sloopy."

It had been one grand run. I hoped that's what Hightower was thinking, if he was thinking anything.

Immediately after the time-out, Hightower whistled OSU's Shannon Scott for an end-line violation. Emphatically, he pointed directly down at the transgressed black strip with the same decisiveness he'd demonstrated in negating Bobby Hansen's game winner thirty years before.

"Hightower, you suck!" This pained cry, provoked by nothing real, was bellowed from the darkened far reaches of the stadium. Or possibly it was just a lingering echo left over from a prior game that ended long, long ago.

Nebraska fought fiercely, despite the impossibility of overcoming a twenty-point deficit in the waning minutes. A few rows behind me, several Nebraska fans started chanting his name, "Hightower, Hightower." Was it a taunt? An accusation? It seemed bizarre, since none of the refs, and certainly not Hightower, had by any stretch of the most paranoid imagination affected the Cornhusker's sorry performance. Could this simply be their warped way of bidding farewell, jacked-up male sports fans expressing affection the only way they knew how, by derisively cackling his name over and over?

But his retirement had not yet been announced (the term itself, "announced," sits awkwardly with regard to the unheralded slipping away that finalizes a ref's career), so that couldn't be it.

Maybe it was just a function of the fact that basketball fans had been watching him seemingly forever, and reviled him with such (misplaced) fervor, that they'd mysteriously, almost telepathically, come to subconsciously intuit his private thoughts and plans, like long-wed couples, even unhappy ones, are said sometimes to do. But I doubted it.

With 3 minutes left, Thad Motta sent in a cascade of substitutes. At the 1:21 mark, Nebraska pulled its starters. Every player on the floor now was a scrub.

With 49 seconds remaining and Ohio State leading 71–50, Hightower called holding on a Nebraska sub. Nobody needed this game to drag on any longer, but there was no dodging it; the kid had slapped way too hard and out of sheer respect for the game, the malfeasance had to be whistled.

For it was all second nature with him by now, right and wrong, allowable and not, fair and unfair, all such distinctions imprinted deeply in his autonomic response system. His face was beaded with perspiration and his eyes, vaguely Asiatic in their tilt, were narrowed to the task at hand. I thought I detected a trace of bemusement in his expression, a slight relaxation of that school principal's façade of sternness, at the silliness of being forced by the Nebraska kid's blunder to blow a pointless whistle when the only issue at stake was his own obligation, shared only by his colleagues, to do this job the right way. His left arm shot chest high as his right arm crossed perpendicularly to clutch the wrist, a hand signal as instinctual as checking his watch for the time.

It was not a shooting foul. He cradled the ball with two hands, as though it were something fragile and might break if dropped, and he carried it to the point on the sideline where Ohio State needed to put it in play.

There was a sudden stirring of discontent among the fans in my section, a breeze kicking up, hinting of foul weather. The outcome of the game had been settled and the natives, not uninfluenced by beer, were growing restless. That was my guess.

I shuddered at what was coming. I had witnessed this scene before, we all have, and it generally does not arrive with a merry smile and a toast to auld lang syne. Mass-audience spectator sports require their red meat, wherever it can be had.

With a surplus of bad guys running roughshod, you'd think we cowards in the grandstand would be grateful to have someone (not us) take on this thankless task of ensuring fairness. Alas, the stalwart sheriff laying down the law in lawless Tombstone was a hero for another era, bygone. Today? Audiences favor those who make a grand display, who take the law into their own hands, loudly, defiantly, emboldened by camera close-ups. "We wuz robbed!" that vintage outcry saturated with self-mockery, had grown into a badge of honor, tantamount to a motto.

It was coming. I could feel the rumbling groundswell.

The final seconds were ticking down.

Sure enough, as predictably as clockwork, the unrest around me ratcheted up. I wasn't sure why except, well, this was a sporting event that had not concluded satisfactorily for all partisans in attendance, and some in the crowd still had energy yet to burn.

Into the dark stadium night, a loud aggrieved male voice thundered forth with that cocksure vehemence that's evolved into something like the mating call of the American sports fan. I quickly turned but could not tell exactly who was squawking out this final harangue, and I guess I didn't need to. It could have been anyone.

"Hightower," the guy hollered with everything he had, "you suck!"

I departed the United Center with that final annoying yelp, "Hightower, you suck," ringing in my ears. It was like a cloying advertising jingle that wouldn't quit. I had a short walk to my car and, based on dire warnings about rampant street crime on Chicago's West Side, I stepped briskly and stayed hyperalert. The March night was dank and nearly cold enough for snow.

Passing the giant bronze sculpture of Michael Jordan raising the ball to the sky in his outsized paw (could it be modeled on the Stature of Liberty?), I couldn't get it out of my head: why would a fan bother flinging one last spitball that had absolutely no relevance to anything that had occurred in the game and had virtually no chance of ever reaching the ears of his intended target? Perhaps the fellow was a mental case who had yet to settle on the appropriate meds for his disorder? That, at least, would be an innocent explanation.

I quickly crossed West Madison to avoid two lanky teenagers in hoodies doing nothing, hands in pockets, not even talking with each other. They could be ball players trolling for a spare ticket to the evening's late game, or something more sinister. Hightower, if he were walking along, would probably approach them, sensing they were not so very different in their confusion and distress from the young athletes he'd made a habit of pulling aside to chastise or console. Growing up in America without many advantages could be tough. He knew. I could imagine him striding straight over to this sullen-looking pair and asking them, point blank, what year they were in school, if they had any favorite subjects, what the homework load was like, and, most essentially, why weren't they doing something more productive with these precious hours of their formative years?

Me, I just walked faster.

Why would that Nebraska fan even bother? Why would anyone go out of his way to rail against invented demons? Weren't there more than enough perfectly legitimate and far more serious problems besetting us, ones with identifiable perpetrators fully deserving of our condemnation?

Of course, that is precisely where spectator sports serve us so very well, as the most surefire, and available, escape from *all that stuff*. Flinging insults at the ref was, I understood, yet another aspect of that yearned-for escape, equally surefire, equally available. No harm, no foul.

I made it safely to my car, a borrowed Toyota, in the parking lot down the street from the United Center. I let the engine run a minute to defrost the windshield. The car warmed. The windshield gradually began to clear. And there it was, staring me in the face, as unmistakable and unanticipated as any last second half-court heave that we're thrilled to watch descend sublimely hoop-ward, so long as our favored team is on the fortunate end.

Hightower had done it! No longer the small boy half-hidden in the deep rows of cotton stalks, no longer the dutiful child in the corner of the classroom waiting to be called on, no longer the promising young athlete whose peak performance, like most of ours, was destined to be imaginary. He'd emerged, finally, as a man whose name was known, and shouted out, by strangers.

Often a scapegoat, to be sure, as referees apparently must be. But not overlooked, not ignored, not shunted aside, not consigned to the shadows, not dismissed, not invisible, not anonymous, not irrelevant, no, not even close to irrelevant.

Initially I'd thought this book could be titled "The Whistleblower" both to highlight that single most emblematic act of officiating, the stop-time toot of the whistle, but mostly to hint at the explosive, tell-all disclosures that would be sure to generate controversy and stimulate sales. The whistle blower who goes on to become, well, you know, a whistleblower!

There was certainly no shortage of topics on which revelations might be forthcoming. College basketball was rife with hot-button controversies about which Hightower, and his fellow refs, probably knew more than they were telling. How could they not? The news pages, and not just the sports pages, periodically produced eye-popping accounts of scandals, each of them seemingly the tip of a very large iceberg that could hardly go unnoticed by smart men who'd proven themselves adept at noticing *everything*.

You had a national championship program (University of Connecticut) getting suspended for recruiting violations. You had Rutgers head coach Mike Rice fired for flagrant abuse, physical and verbal, of his players. You had an elite AAU team in Houston run by a Ponzi-scheming businessman who'd been investing money on behalf of prominent college coaches who'd conveniently recruited his athletes. You had the perfectly legal yet ethically dubious phenomenon of talented high schoolers entering college as freshmen with an all but explicit understanding that one year, even as little as one full academic semester, one-and-done as it's known, was all that would be expected of them before graduating to the pros. If the average fan had become aware of all of these travesties, how much more must the keen referee know?

The mistreatment of the young athletes was a matter about which I felt certain Hightower had strong feelings. The misleading promises that get made just to sign a high school prospect, the failure to provide adequate academic support and counseling, the preposterous grade inflation that occasionally spills over to outright fraud, the financial hardships exacerbated by the relative prosperity of the general campus population, the risk of serious injury and the conflicted allegiance of medical advisors, the fickle conditionality of the scholarship itself — all yours when things are good, swiftly withdrawn when they are not — were all affronts to the very values Hightower most honored.

I'd seen him roll his eyes at some of the pieties that get flaunted — the nobility of our grand tradition of the student-athlete, the timeless glories of amateurism, the immense academic benefits trickling down to the general education of the student body from successful sports teams. I knew he had his reservations. I knew he believed the system was imperfect. For all these reasons, he was, in theory, absolutely ripe to be a whistleblower. The stage was set.

I'd pressed Hightower to name names. I'd cajoled him to spill the beans.

To say he was uninterested is a severe understatement. It was not going to happen. "The game of basketball," he always insisted, "has been better to me than I have been to it."

Well, sure. Still, I struggled to convince him by resorting to that textbook reporter's methodology for inducing a source to talk. Think of all the good that might be accomplished, I argued. Think of all the improvements that might result. Think of the quality and the character of the game.

He cut me off. The quality and character of college basketball? Yes, he certainly did care about that. And he had proven it through his performance in over one thousand games, time and again, in the only way that he or any referee realistically ever can. He had done all that was within his power, marshaling his best energies and maximizing his accumulated wisdom, night after night after night, to ensure that the team that played the best over the course of the game enjoyed a fair shot at winning. That's what we needed him for. More than that, no referee can possibly do.

And like those fiercely competitive and unyielding athletic heroes we so admire, Ed Hightower had left it all, the very best he had to offer, on the court.

ACKNOWLEDGMENTS

In the course of researching this book I spoke with a number of working referees whose names do not appear in the preceding chapters because they preferred not to be identified. There is a general belief among referees that, like behind-the-scenes diplomats engaged in back-channel negotiations, they can be most successful in their mission if they are not perceived as desiring any personal attention beyond what is, by the nature of their work, unavoidable. The call not to be quoted or cited was entirely theirs, and I will not challenge it.

Except to say, this preference for relative anonymity, surely an anomaly in our age of rampant self-promotion, is a characteristic so admirable on the face of it I'm tempted to single them out and salute them simply for that impulse alone. But I won't.

First and foremost, I am grateful to Ed Hightower. He made time in his demanding schedule for my inquiries and used his influence, in ways that occasionally inconvenienced him, to get me a box seat for some of the action.

Members of the Hightower family were gracious with their recollections. Ed's wife, Barbara, his mother, Daisy, his daughters, Jennifer and Julie, and three of his brothers, Clarence, Calvin, and Robert, were all helpful. Each in their own way told me details that proved useful and revealing. Just as importantly, the keen intelligence and generosity of spirit that infused their conversation reinforced my impression of an extraordinary family rooted in exceptional values.

Lee Stevens, a basketball aficionado who is also a product of the pre-civil-rights-era Missouri Bootheel region, escorted me to a Buckeyes game in Columbus and enlightened me about Ed Hightower and the art of officiating. It was Lee who confided that he primarily watches the refs when he watches a college basketball game. Learning this encouraged me to think that, with his tutelage, I might give it a try.

Doug Wilhide, poet, essayist, and friend from an undergraduate experience that included both the writing seminar that first encouraged me to take it, as the pros say, "to the next level," and an erratic intramural basketball team that occasionally let me shoot, reviewed a draft of the manuscript and contributed many worthy suggestions. His notes to me in the loose-leaf margins, hand-scrawled in no. 2 pencil, were often as difficult to decipher as a doctor's prescription, and just as welcome. Even when I failed to solve the mystery of exactly what Doug had written, I felt I was sufficiently familiar with his editorial preferences to make the corrections I figured he was suggesting.

Will Anderson, a historian by instinct and a college basketball fan (Badgers) by compulsion, provided research assistance that, fortunate for me, was coupled with valuable insights. Louis Katz helped with research and served as a contrarian sounding board on a few matters that properly did not make the final cut.

Several friends provided the kind of companionable conversations that allowed me to incubate and sharpen my thoughts about this book, and granted tacit permission to slyly annex a few of their thoughts as well. In particular, Martin Lee, Jeff Cohen, and Doug Melton at various stages helped me recognize what was most interesting about this material, and helped me clarify ways to spell it out. Norman Zamcheck, who knows next to nothing about sports, was nonetheless, and perhaps for that very reason, a source of enlightened feedback.